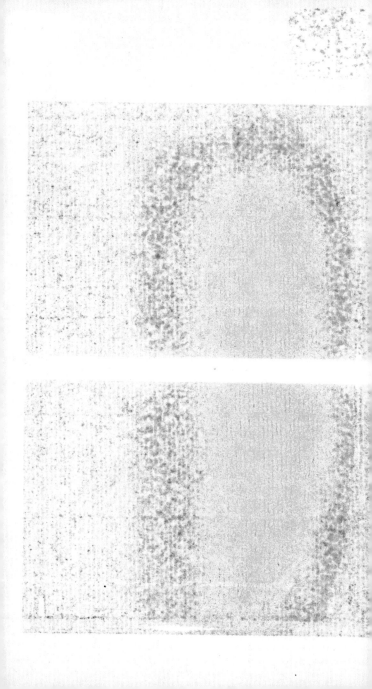

ENGLISH RECUSANT LITERATURE
1558–1640

Selected and Edited by
D. M. ROGERS

Volume 300

PEDRO DE RIBADENEIRA
The Life of B. Father Ignatius
1616

PEDRO DE RIBADENEIRA

The Life of B. Father Ignatius of Loyola
1616

The Scolar Press
1976

ISBN 0 85967 301 4

Published and printed in Great Britain by
The Scolar Press Limited, 59-61 East Parade,
Ilkley, Yorkshire and
39 Great Russell Street,
London WC1

1912962

NOTE

Reproduced (original size) from a copy in the Community Library, Mount Street, London, by permission of the Librarian.

References: Allison and Rogers 712; STC 20967.

THE LIFE
OF B. FATHER
IGNATIVS
OF LOYOLA,

Authour, and Founder of the
Society of IESVS.

Translated out of Spanish into English,
By W. M. of the same Society.

Extendit palmites suos vsque ad mare : & vsque
ad flumen propagines eius. Psal. 79.

Permissu Superiorum. M. DC. XVI.

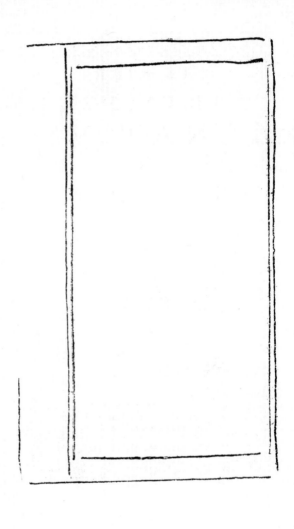

TO
THE TRVLY
HONOVRABLE
AND
VERTVOVS
GENTLE-WOMAN
Mʳˢ Anne Vaux.

RIGHT VER-
TVOVS,

*HAVING transla-
ted, & being now to publish this briefe
History of the Blessed man* F. Ignatius

of Loyola; *I could not doubt, but that it would be gratefull to* YOV, *who haue deserued so well of his Children liuing in our afflicted Country. And therfore my choyce was soone made of your Self, before all others, to direct this my small labour vnto: which indeed is so small, that vnlesse the matter which it coteyneth were esteemed, it were not worth the offering to any. Wherfore you must not thanke me, but your owne vertuous Disposition, if you take any contentment therein.*

To which (if you will needes haue some other to partake with you) that Worthie and Reuerend Man Father Peter Ribadeneyra, *who is the Author, deserueth best to be added, being in a maner from his Childhood brought vp in the Religious Schoole of the forsaid Blessed Father, & continued therin, with great edification, aboue* 70.

ycares;

yeares: and among his many pious and
profitable labours, was very eminent for
his writings, eſpecially in the Spaniſh
Tongue, as is welbknowne to all of that
nation, by his many deuout & learned
Treatiſes which are extant. But aboue
all other, by thoſe which appertayne to
Hiſtory, among which our Nation was
not forgotten; for he tranſlated & aug-
mented D. Saunders Bookes, Of our
Engliſh Schiſme, beginning with
King Henry the VIII. who vpon the
foule occaſiō, which the world knoweth,
was the firſt cauſe therof, and proſecu-
ting the ſame vnto the later dayes of
Queene Elizabeth.

He alſo wrote with great cōmenda-
tions the Liues of all the Saints which
are ſet downe in the Roman Calendar,
and of diuers others. By occaſion of
which he publiſhed this briefe Narratiō
of Bleſſed Father Ignatius, which I

A 3   haue

haue translated; wherein, as in an A-
bridgment, he, in few wordes, com-
prehendeth that which he had set down
more at large in a former Treatise, and
withall inferted many notable miracles,
which had byn wrought by this Holy
Man; for the most part, after the edition
of his former booke. And yet he relateth
not all: for God hath since that time lik-
wife continued to manifest the great
fanctity of this Blessed Father by many
more, in diuers parues of the Christian
world. I will only make mention of one,
which hath byn published in print, and
happened in the Prouince of Perù, and
in the Citty of Lima, of which I make
choice, the rather, because the occasion
therof was taken by reading of those,
which are recited in this Relation.

In the Conuent of S. Dominike in
the forsayd Citty there was a Religious
man of that Order, named Father Al-

uarus de Molina, *a man of good ac-count, and only hindred from great im-ploiments by long & continuall ſicknes:* for he had byn moleſted with a dead pal-ſy for the ſpace of ten yeares; eight of which he had likewiſe ſo terrible a con-vulſion, as the Phiſitians call it, that he could not moove his body, nor goe one ſteppe, nor lift his handes to his head, nor almoſt ſpeake any word that could be vnderſtood. The Phiſitians & Sur-geons had giuen him ouer, accounting his diſeaſe incurable. Wherefore the good Father conforming his wil to that of God, ſpent moſt of his tyme in praying & reading ſpirituall bookes, for which he needed ſome helpe, not being able to turne ouer the leaues himſelf.

Hauing ended one of thoſe deuout bookes, he deſired F. Iames de Ojeda, a Religious mã of the ſame Order, to pro-cure him another, which he willingly

vnder-

vndertooke, & made choyce of this our
History, giuing great comendatiō therof. The other accepted it very willingly,
& hauing read the Miracles coteyned
therein, he conceiued so great deuotion
to B.F. Ignatius, & had such firme cōfidēce in his intercession, that he made
a vow to fast his Vigil, or Eue, so long as
he liued, & to make a Comemoration of
him twice euery day, besides other deuotiōs which he would always vse towards
him, togeather with a particuler affectiō & good will to his Order, if it pleased God to restore his health & strēgth
by the prayers of this holy man. This
vow caused him extraordinary cōfort,
& so he renewed it dayly, vntil it pleasedGod to renew & restore him his former health and strength, which he did
within lesse then a fortnight, after the
first making thereof, in manner following.

Vpon

Vpon the 8. day of Nouēber, which is the Octaue of All-Saints, in the yeare of our Lord 1607. betweene 4. & 5. of the clock in the afternoone, Father Aluarus sitting in his chayre, as he was allwayes wont when he was out of his bed, felt within himself an inward impulsion or motion, and as it were a prayer, which incauraged him & sayd: Rise vp, & walke; & this was with so great delight and satisfaction, that he stood vp, and began to goe: and finding himself strong & able, he went downe a payre of stayres, where he met with many that came from an Act of Diuinity, who did all wonderfully admyre to see him goe in that manner. To whome he related his vow, & how it had pleased God to cure him thus perfectly by the intercession of B. Father Ignatius.

By which narration of his, they discouered yet more plainly the greatnesse

A 5   of

of the Miracle: for wheras before ſcarce any word he ſayd could be vnderſtood, ſo that it was neceſſary to make him repeate the ſame thing often, & to go very neere vnto him; now there was no ſuch difficulty at all, for he ſpake very clearly & diſtinctly. The Religious men of that houſe, ſeeing ſo euidēt a Miracle, went preſently into the Church, and F. Aluarus with them, who hauing proſtrated himſelfe before the Bleſſed Sacrament, the reſt ſung Te Deum laudamus, *with Muſike and Organs: which being done, they ſent word of all to the Colledge of the Society of* Ieſus, *diuers Religious men of S. Dominiks Order going thither to congratulate with them, affirming that this Miracle had as many witneſſes, as there were Religious men in their houſe, & that it was ſo euidēt, that the Diuel himſelf could not calumniate it: ſo that it alone*

were

were ſufficient to moue any Gentile to
belieue, that the Catholike Romane
fayth is the true Religion, and that B.
Father Ignatius *is a Saint.*

The Phiſitians alſo did affirme with
one conſent, that it was a manifeſt Mi-
racle, and Father Aluarus *his diſ-*
eaſe was ſo notorious, that a thouſand
wittneſſes might eaſily haue byn found
to affirme the ſame. It was ſtrange to
ſee, what wonderfull Ioy, Deuotion,
and Admiration this Miracle cauſed
in all that Citty. God grant we may
diſpoſe our ſelues to find the like effects,
which wee may the more eaſily ob-
tayne, if we help our ſelues with the
Holy interceſſion of Bleſſed Father
Ignatius. *From the reading of whoſe*
hiſtory, I will not detayne you any lon-
ger, but earneſtly entreat you to be
mindfull of me in your deuout prayers,
& particulerly in thoſe which you make

to

The Epistle Dedicatory,

to this Glorious Patriarch . Which request I likewise make to all others, who shall reape any benefit by this my small labour . And so I end, and rest, This feast of All-Saintes 1615.

Yours euer assured,

VV . M.

T H E

THE

TABLE OF THE

CHAPTERS.

him

of

THE TABLE.

B. Fa-

THE

THE LIFE
OF B. IGNATIVS
OF LOYOLA,
Founder of the Society of Iesvs.

Of the Birth and Lineage of Ignatius : and of his Conuersion from a secular life.

CHAP. I.

BLESSED Father Ignatius of Loyola Founder, and Father of the Society of IESVS, was borne in that part of Spaine, which is called

the

the Prouince of Guipuzcoa, the
yeare of our Lord 1491. Pope
Innocentius 8. fitting in the
chayre of S. Peter, and Frede-
ricke the third being Emperour, and Don Ferdinandus
with Doña Ifabella of glorious
memory gouerning the Catholike Kingdome of Spayne. His
Father was named Beltram
Iagnez, Lord of Ognez and
Loyola, and head of that Ho-
nourable and Ancient family.
His Mother was named Ma-
ria Sonez of Balda, daughter
to the Lords of the Houfe
and Teritory of Balda, a Matron equall to her husband
both in birth and nobility.
Thefe two houfes of Loyola
and Balda are of thofe which
are called Great, and of the

most

moſt principall in the Prouince of Guipuzcoa.

2. Our Ignatius from
his child-hood diſcouered a
quick, ſharp, and great wit;
and after ſome few yeares he
was ſent to the Catholike
Kings Court, that he might
there be brought vp amóg his
Equalls. His courage increa-
ſing with his age, he gaue
himſelfe earneſtly to all manner of warlike exerciſe, that
he might obtayne the reputa-
tion of being valiant, and of
military honor and glory.

3. It happened that in the
yeare 1521. the Frenchmen be-
ſieging the Caſtle of Pampelona, Ignatius entred into it
with the Captaynes and ſouldiers, that were appointed

for the defence thereof. The
siege being very straite, and
they who were within, ha-
uing no hope of succour, began to treat of a composition,
and had concluded it, if Ignatius had not opposed him-
selfe, incouraging them to resist the enemy vntill death.
But the French men conti-
nuing their battery of the
Castle, while Ignatius defended it, he was wounded with
a bullet in his right legge, so
that the bones thereof were
not only broken, but also shi-
uered in peeces: and besides a
stone being driuen out of the
wall with the force of the
bullet, had also sorely hurt his
left legge. Ignatius being thus
ouerthrowne, the rest were

dif-

e is
ounded in
e defence of
e castle
Pamplona.

difcomfited, & yielded themfelues to the French, who carying Ignatius to their Tents,
and vnderftanding who he
was, caufed him to be very
carefully looked vnto; and
after fent him home in a litter
vpon mens fhoulders.

4. His ficknes increafed
in fuch fort, that there was
little hope of his life: but our
Lord releeued him in his
greateft danger, fending vnto
him the moft glorious Prince
of the Apoftles S. Peter, to
whom he had euer byn very
deuout, vpon the Eue of his
Feaft: and he appeared vnto
him as one, who came to fauour him, & reftore his health.
With this vifitatiō of the holy
Apoftle our fouldier began to

S. Peter
appea-
reth vn-
him, and
refto-
reth his
health.

B 3 waxe

wax better, and to recouer his
health: but defiring to become
a Gallant, and to follow the
neateft and fineftfafhions, he
caufed a bone. which remayned fticking out deformedly
vnder his knee to be cut of ,
that fo he might (as I haue
heard him fay) draw on a
ftraite boot. Neyther wouldhe
be bound while it was a doing
efteeming it a thing vnworthy of his noble mind . And
though the paine were ex-
treme, & very fharp (becaufe
they were to cut into the
quick) yet he kept his countenance, and fhewed fuch courage , as caufed admiration ,
neuer changing colour , nor
once fighing or fpeaking any
word , which might difcouer

any

any weaknes, as he had done
before in all the reſt of his
cure.

5. In the tyme of his re-
couery lying in his bed, and
being accuſtomed to read
prophane books of Chiualry,
he asked for ſome ſuch vayne
Treatiſe, to paſſe the tyme
withall, which ſeemed long,
and tedious. They brought
him two bookes, one of the
Life of Chriſt, and the other
of the Liues of Saints, there
being none of thoſe others
which he would haue had in
the houſe. Wherefore he began to read in theſe at the beginning, that he might paſſe
away the tyme, but afterward
he tooke great delight and af
fection therin : and our Lord

He is cõ
uerted
by rea-
ding th
liues of
Saints.

B 4 wrought

wrought so farre in the hart
of Ignatius with that reading,
that he was changed, conceauing a desire to imitate that
which he read. So, that though
he foūd great repugnáce, many contentions and grieuous
combats within himselfe, becaufe his long and inueterate
cuftome, and the fubtilties
& tentations of Sathan were
of great force to detayne him
in the world; yet notwithftāding Grace preuayled againft
corruption of nature, and the
Comfort of heauen againft
the tyrány of his former euill
life, and the fauour of God
who had chofen him for great
matters, againft all the crafts,
and deceipts of the enemy,
Wherefore one night rifing

out

out of his bed (as he was
often wont)to pray , & kneeling downe before a picture
of our B. Lady, with humble
and feruent confidēce, he offered himselfe by the meanes
of this glorious Mother , to
her bountifull and mercifull
Sonne, for his faythfull fouldier and feruant, promifing
him to follow his Enfigne
and to forfake the world .

Of the feruour of his pennance,
and contempt of the world.

CHAP. II.

AT the very tyme, that he
made this prayer , there
was a very great noyfe heard
in all the houfe , and the

chamber where he was did shake, and a glasse window in it was broken. In this his change of life he greatly feared the weakenes of his flesh, but the most sacred Virgin, and most soueraigne Queene of the Angells (to whom he most deuoutly commended himselfe) appeared vnto him one night while he was awake, with her most pretious Sonne in her arms, by meanes of which heauenly visitatiõ our Lord gaue him such great grace, and changed him in that manner, cleansing his soule from all filthy, and dishoneft delight, that from that inftant to the end of his life, he remayned pure and chaft, without any spot, in great

Our B. Lady appeareth vnto him with our Sauiour in her armes, and giueth him the gift of chaftity.

inte-

integrity, and freedome.

2. He fought to imbrace that ftate and manner of life, in which he might afflict his body with more rigour & pénance, and find God more perfectly. To this end he determined to forfake his houfe, kindred, and acquaintance; which he did, his elder brother Martin Garcia of Loyola not being able to diffwade him to the contrary: and by occafion of vifiting the Duke of Najara, he went to our B. Ladyes of Montferat attended by two men, whom he fent back by the way, giuing them part of that which he had.

3. From the day that he departed from home, he vfed euery night to make a fharp difci-

He goeth to Montferat, an difcipli neth himfel euery night.

discipline, which he continued al his iourney: and being
inflamed in the loue of God,
and burning with zeale of his
honour, he now referred all
that he did, & purposed to do,
TO GODS GREATER GLORY
for this was alway, as it were
the Poesy of Ignatius, and the
soul, and life of all his workes.
Likewise in this iourney he
made a vow of chastity, and
offered to Christ our Lord the
purity of his soule and body,
with singular deuotion, and a
feruent desyre to obtayn it, as
he did, in that entyre & com-
plete manner, which we haue
already mentioned.

He ma-
keth a
vow of
chastity.

4 In a Village not far from
Môtserat he bought him a garment, or habit, which he pur-

poſed to weare in the Pilgrimage which he intended to
Hieruſalem : and this was a
coate of ſackcloth , or courſe
canuaſe, down to the foot, and
a cord for his girdle , a payn of
country buskyns, a little botle,
and a Pilgrims ſtaffe .

5. Comming to that Holy
place of our B. Lady at Montſe-
rat, the firſt thing he did was to
ſeeke (as a ſick man who deſi-
reth health) the beſt Phiſitian,
and Confeſſarius which he
could find , to diſcouer his
wounds vnto him . He found a
Holy religious man of the
French nation called Fr. Iohn
Clanon, a great ſeruant of God, He ma-
known, & reuerenced for ſuch. keth a
With this good Father, Ignatius generall
made a generall Confeſſion of côfeſſiô.
all

all his life for the space of three
dayes, with great diligence, remorse, and feeling of his sins:
And this religious man was the
first to whom he opened his
purposes, and intents, as to his
spirituall Father, and Maister.
He gaue his horse to the Monastery, and caused his sword, and
dagger with which he had serued the world before to be hanged vp at our B. Ladies Altar,
seeking other new & more resplendent weapons to serue our
Lord withall.

6. To this end vpon the
Eue of that ioyfull, and most
glorious day, the 25. of March,
in which the eternal Word clad
himself with our flesh in the
womb of his most pure Mother
the yeare 1522. very secretly in

the

the night he went to a poore
Pilgrim, altogether destitute of
apparell, which was there, and
putting of all his cloathes (vnto
his shirt) he gaue him them, &
cloathed himselfe with that his
desired sackcloth which he had
bought, and with much deuotion placed himselfe before the
Altar of the B. Virgin, where he
remayned all that night, partly
standing, and partly kneeling,
to watch like a new knight of
Christ those his new and in ap-
pearance poore, & weake weapons, but indeede very rich,
and strong, commending himselfe earnestly to the protection
of the most Sacred Virgin, be-
wayling his sinnes most bitterly, and purposing to amend
them with her fauour.

He wat-
cheth
his wea-
pons af-
ter the
manner
of new
soul-
diers.

7. In

7. In the morning before it was day, that he might not be knowne, he departed in great haste towards a towne called Manresa, which standeth at the foote of the mountayn three leagues from Montserat, and somewhat out of the high way to Barcelona. In this manner Ignatius went ioyfull being clad with that poore, and course sackcloth, girded with a cord, carrying his pilgrims staff in his hand, without any hat, and wearing a shoo but vpon one foot only, which seemed necessary, because that leg was yet weake, and not thoroughly recouered, in so much that it swelled a new euery night. But this his ioy was presently diminished

by

by the comming of one to de-
mand of him, whether it were
true, that he had giuen his rich
apparell to a poore mā, whom
the officers had apprehended,
suspecting, least he had stoln
them. By this means he was
enforced to tel the truth, to deliuer him that was innocent,
and he shed many teares, thinking himself to great a sinner,
that he could not so much as
help his neighbour without
doing him harm, and putting
him to shame. And though
they asked him his Name,
who he was, and also from
whence he came, yet he answered them to none of these
questions, thinking that there
was no cause why he should,
and desyring to be vnknown,

and deſpiſed in the eyes of the world.

8. In Manreſa he went directly to the hoſpitall of S. Lucie, that he might lyue on almes among the poore. He began to afflict, and waſt his body with a very ſharp, and rigorous life, & to mortify al the delights & vayne cares which he had before. And becauſe he had bin curious in the world in trymming his hayre, and adorning his perſon, now he went bareheaded night and day, neuer vſing combe, or any thing els therto: and with the ſame contempt of himſelf he ſuffered his nayles, & beard to grow out of order. He had no other bed but the ground, watching in a manner all the

night,

night, weeping bitterly for
his sinns. He vsed after this to
make three austere disciplynes
euery day, and prayed 7. ho-
wers vpon his knees, and all
this with as great deuotion, &
feruour as he could.

9. He heard Masse, Euen-
song, and Complyn euery day
with great comfort, and contentment of his mynd, which
being tender in deuotion had
eassly imprinted in it such diuine things; and those voices,
and praises of our Lord pierced to the inmost of his soul.
He did vse to eat but once a
day a little bread, & therwith
drank a litle water, which was
giuen vnto him of almes, & he
fasted all the weeke in this
manner except the Sundayes,

vpon which he went to confeſſion, & receyued the moſt
Holy ſacrament of the Altar.

10. He was ſo deſyrous to
mortiſie his fleſh and to bring
it to the obedience; and ſub-
iection of the ſpirit, that he depriued himſelf of all things
which could giue any delight
to his body, by which meanes
though he were a ſtrong man,
and of great forces, yet in few
dayes, he came to be very
weak, with the rigour of ſuch
auſtere pennance.

How

How he is freed of Scrupulosity & enioyeth diuine Reuelations. And of the Monument erected in his honour at Manresa.

CHAP. III.

NEYTHER did this outward Pennance, and affliction of his body weaken him so much, as the inward scruples, & anxietyes which tormented his spirit. For though he had with all diligence, and care made a generall Confession of his synnes as we haue said; yet our Lord, who by this way would wash, and purg him from them, afflicted him in such sort with

the remorfe of confcience, and
that gnawing worme which
did eat, and teare his hart, that
he found no reft in prayer, nor
eafe in fafting, and watching
nor remedy in his difciplynes
and other Pennances ; but
deiected as it were with the
force of fadneffe , and dif-
maide, and difcouraged with
the violence of that extreme
griefe , he proftrated himfelf
on the ground , as one that
were ouerwhelmed, & drow-
ned with the waues and bil-
lowes of the fea . This trouble
wēt fo far , that hauing almoft
loft himfelf, and being defo-
late of all comfort, he refolued
neyther to eat , nor drink vntill he found the defyred peace
of his foule, vnleffe he fhould

happen

happen to be in danger of death .

2. And with this purpofe he remayned feauen whole dayes, without tafting any thing, not omitting for all this his feauen houres of prayer vpon his knees, and his three difciplins euery day, togeather with the other exercifes & deuotions which he was wont to vfe, vntill giuing accompt to his Confeffarius what he had done, and how he purpofed to go forward, was commaunded by him in Gods name to take fome thing : to whome he obeyed, though he found himfelf to haue his accuftomed forces, and nothing weakened. By this obedience and for the entyre affection, &

aboun-

aboundant teares with which
he beseeched his Diuyne Maiesty, our Lord vouchsafed to
comfort his seruant, and to
illustrate him with new light
from Heauen , giuing him a
wonderfull peace and serenity
in his soule, and such an admirable discretion of spirits, that
there scarce euer repayred to
him afterward any scrupulous
person , tormented with this
infirmity , who was not deliuered by his counsayle. Neither did he only enrich him
with this so notable a fauour ,
but likewise cōforted his spirit with soueraigne, and maruelous Visitatiōs from Heauē,
(as shalbe sayd hereafter)
that according to the measure
of the former sorowes which

God gi-
ueth
him
peace &
discretiō
of spirits.

he

he had endured , *the consolati-*
ons of our Lord might (as the
Prophet saith) *refresh , and re-*
ioyce his soule.

3 . The light which our
Lord gaue to this his seruant
euen in those beginnings, and
the care which he tooke in the
courses, by which God directed him , were so great, that
being (as he was) a man vntill
that tyme giuen to the noise
and vanity of war, and so vn-
learned , that he could only
write and read : in this very
tyme he wrote the booke
which we call the *Spiritual Ex-*
ercises, which is so replenished
with documents, & excellent
instructions in spirituall matters, that it clearly appeareth,
how the vnction of the holy

C 5   Ghost

Ghoſt taught him & ſupplied
the want , which at that time
he had of ſtudy & learning.
For it cãnot eaſely be thought,
how much fruit theſe haue
taken by this booke, who haue
exerciſed themſelues in the
meditations & rules, that are
in it ; and what profit hath
enſued in the whole Catholik
Church, aſwell in religious, as
ſecular people by the vſe of
theſe Exerciſes. This book after much examination , Pope
Paul the third of happy memory confirmed with his A-
poſtolick authority, by his letters dated the yeare 1548 .in
which he exhorteth all the
faithfull to read them, and to
exerciſe themſelues in the meditations , and rules which

they

He wri-
teth the
booke
of exer-
ciſe .

they containe; as may be seene
at large in his Breue, which
goeth printed with the booke
it selfe of the said Exercises.

4. But our Ignatius being
so seuere towards himself, and
not remiting any thing of the
rigour of his austerity & pennance, broken with the ex-
cessiue labors of body, & continuall combats of mynd, fell
into a very grieuous sicknes:
in which the Inhabitans of
Manresa prouided him of all
necessaryes with much charity, and many honest, and
deuout persons serued, and attended him with the same; for
they accounted, and esteemed
him as a Saint. And the deuotion which they of that place
coceaued towards him was so

great

great, that it being now almoſt 80. yeares ſince this paſſed, there is at this day in Mā-
reſa a very freſh memory, and
great ſignes of the life which
he lead there: and thoſe of that
Citty do very piouſly frequēt
the places where he liued, and
vſed to pray, crauing our
Lords fauour by his interceſſion. And for a perpetuall remembrance thereof, Doctor
Iohn Baptiſta Cardona, Biſhop of Vich (in whoſe Dio-
ceſſe Manreſa is ſituated) and
Lord Elect of Iortoſa, cauſed
a Pirameſſe of ſtone to be e-
erected in Manreſa at the
Church of S. Lucie, which
was before an hoſpitall of
poore people, where Ignatius
founder of the Society of

IESVS

IESVS beganne to do pennance, with an Inscription : which becaufe it is a particuler thinge , and declareth greatly the opinion , and eftimation which they haue in that Country of the holyneffe of our Father , 1 haue thought it not amiffe to tranflate it out of Latin, and recite it in this place . And this it is .

5. *To Ignatius of Loyola the fonne of Beltram of the Prouince of Guipuzcoa Founder of the Society of Iefus, who being of the age of 30. yeares , in the caftle of Pampelona fought valiantly with the French-men for the defence of his country: and hauing receaued fome mortall woundes , and being recouered of them, by Gods*

fingu-

The pyrameffe of Man refa.

singular benefit, enflamed with a
desyre to visit the Holy Places of
Hierusalem, he tooke his iourney
making a vow of chastity: and leauing the weapons, which (as a
souldier) he was wont to weare,
hanged vp in the Church of our
B. Lady of Montserat, cloathed
in sack, and hayrecloth, and al
most naked, he began to bewaile
the synns of his former life in this
place, and as a new souldier of
Christ to take reuenge of himselfe
with fastings, teares, and praiers.

For the memory of so worthy
a thing, and the glory of God, and
honour and renowne of his Society, Iohn Baptista Cardona borne
in Valentia, Bishop of Vich, and
Elected of Iortosa, for the great
deuotion which he beareth to the
sanctity of the said Father, and

of

of his Order, caufed this ftone to be
erected as to a moft pious man,
and to whom the whole Chriftian
Common wealth is fo much indeb-
ted: Sixtus *Quintus* being Pope,
and the Catholike, and great Philip the fecond of that name King
of Spaine .

How he went to Rome, & thence
to Hierufalem: And what
happened vnto him in this
his Pilgrimage .

CHAP. IIII.

BEING a little recouered,
he prefently returned to
his accuftomed penances, and
fo fell downe agayne the fecond, and third tyme; for
with an vnwearyed, and per-

feuerant mind he tooke vpon him a heauyer burden then his forces could beare. But in the end ouercome by his owne experience, and with an extreme payne of his ftomake, which tormented him, togeather with the afperity of winter, by the counfaile of his deuout friends, he tooke two fhort coates of courfe ruffet cloth to keep his body warme, and a little cap of the fame cloth to weare vpon his head.

2. Our Ignatius ftayed almoft a yeare in Manrefa, leading the life, which we haue related : but our Lord who had ordayned him for greater matters, tooke him out of that folitude, infpiring him to go, and vifit the holy

places

places of Hierusalem. To this
intent he departed from Man
resa, and went alone to Barcelona, without taking any
other company with him but
that of God, with whom he
desired to treat by himselfe,
and to enioy his inward com-
municatiō, without noyse, or
hinderance of others, though
many had offered themselues
to accompany him in that
iourney. And likewise be-
cause he would wholy de-
pend of the Fatherly prouidence of God, without rely-
ing, or putting his confidence
in any creature. In Barcelona
he went to the Church to
heare a sermon, & sate downe
among the litle children vpon
the steps of the Altar. There

He goo-
eth to
Hierusa-
lem.

D   was

was present a Lady called E-
lizabeth Rosell, who beholding our Pilgrim, seemed (as
shee tould me herselfe afterward in Rome) to perceaue a
light, and splendour in his
countenance, and that she

His coū-
tenance
becom-
meth
resplen-
dent.

heard in her hart, as it were a
voyce, which said vnto her,
Call him, Call him. And so she
did at the end of the Sermon,
& inuited him to dinner with
her husband, who was blind,
all in the house meruailing
much at his words, modesty,
and the spirit with which he
spake of Diuine things, & exhorted them to loue the chiefest good with all diligence.

3. This Lady hindred
him from going in a little
ship, with which he had al-

ready

ready agreed, and it was after
caſt away in the ſight of Barcelona, and ſhe procured him
paſſage in a great ſhip, which
with ſtrõg, & boiſtrous winds
went from Barcelona to Gaj-
eta in fiue daies; from whence
he departed towards Rome
with great labour, & difficulty. For this yeare (being that
of 1523.) Italy was much infected with the plague, and
for this cauſe he was not permitted to enter into the
Towns: ſo that the hunger,
& weaknes which he ſuffred
was ſo great, that not being
able to go one ſtep further,
he was inforced to ſtay where
the night ouertooke him. But
at laſt, as well as he could ſõ-
tyms falling, & riſing againe

he

he arriued at Rome vpon Palme-Sunday, and visited with great deuotion the sacred Stations, & sanctuaryes of that holy Citty, and likewise obtayned the benedictiō of Pope Adrian the sixt, who at that tyme was the Chiefe Pastor of Gods Church.

4. He remayned a fortnight in Rome, and though many endeauoured to alter his purpose of going to Hierusalem, by proposing vnto him the great labours, dangers, and difficultyes which were incident to that long iourney in a yeare of such dearth, and sicknes; yet they could make no impression in him. Only they persuaded him to take 7. or 8. crowns, which

they

they gaue him at his departure
to pay for his shipping, and
passage: which afterward hauing remorse of conscience &
thinking that it was not agre-
able to the spirit of true pouerty, which he desired to follow
in all things, he distributed
al the said money to the poore
that he met vpon the way.
In which he endured incredi-
ble afflictions, being put back
from the townes, lying in the
fields; all those who met him
flying from him, no lesse then
from death it selfe: because
they did see him so pale and
wan, and forsaken by those
who went along the same
way.

5. But our Lord (who
said, I will not forsake, nor

Iosue 1.

D 3   leaue

Being alone, & desolate IESVS Christ appeareth vnto him.

leaue thee,) vouchsafed to visit him, as he went from Choca to Padua in a playne field, comforting him with his sweet, and soueraigne presence, and encouraging him to endure harder things for his sake, after which he found more easy entrance into Padua, and Venice, where he would not speake with the Embassadour, who for the Emperour Charles the King of Spayne was Legier in that Common wealth. For he sought not any humane, but the diuine fauour. In Venice he had new difficulties, and feares to dismay, and hinder him from this iourney, because the Great Turke Soliman had taken the Ile of

Rhodes

des the yeare before, and by reason of the sicknes, and agues which he had in that place: but nothing was sufficient to debate our Pilgrims courage, nor to diminish the secure, and firme confidence, with which he had settled in his hart, that if only one ship were to passe that yeare to Hierusalem, yet our Lord would procure him passage therin.

6. Being in venice, he asked his meat of almes from dore to dore according to his custome, and in the night he lay in the publick market place of S. Marke, which is the chiefest of that Citty. But one night a Senatour, and one of the most principall of

D 4   that

A Senator admonished by God, seeketh, & findeth him lying vpon the ground.

that Citty sleeping in his bed with much commodity, and ease, heard a voyce which awakened him, and sayd: *How art thou so daintily, and richly clad, and liuest with so many commodities in thy house, whilst my Seruant remayneth naked in the streets? Thou sleepest in a rich, and soft bed, and he lyeth abroad vpon the hard ground.* The Senator being astonished at this voyce, riseth out of his bed, and in great hast goeth out of his house, vp and downe the streetes, and comming to S. Marks, he findeth our Pilgrim lying vpon the ground, and vnderstanding him to be the man, whom our Lord comanded him to seeke, he carieth

him

him that night to his houſe,
& vſeth him with much courteſy. But he, being deſirous
to auoyd ſuch delicacies and
honour, went to a Spaniards
houſe, an old acquaintance of
his, who by many intreaties
had inuited him thither. After
this he ſpake to Andrew Gri-
ti, who at that tyme was ᴅuke
of Venice, and deſired him to
commaund, that he might
haue ſhipping. The Duke
granted, commanding that he
ſhould be caryed of free coſt
to Cyprus in the Captaynes
ſhip in which the new gouernour himſelfe went.

7. The 14. day of Iuly of
the ſame yeare 1523. he went
aboard, and departed from
Venice, hauing immediatly

He ta-
keth
ſhip for
Hieruſa-
lem, and
God cō-
forteth
him and
deliue-
reth him
from a
great
danger

D 5   before

before taken a Purgation
by reason a of great ague,
which at that very tyme had
assayled him : and yet Phisitians tould him, that if he tooke
ship that day he would put his
life in manifest danger. But
he being inwardly guided by
an other superiour Phisitian
made no account of that
which they sayd, and indeed
his going to sea was the cause
of his perfect recouery.

8. In this ship wherin he
went there were great sins &
wickednes committed, which
our Pilgrim inflamed with
the zeal and loue of God, reprehended with great liberty,
so that the Mariners taking
this in ill part, determined to
leaue him in a desolate, and

vnhabited

vnhabited Iland . But at the
very tyme that they came to
it, a fuddaine & furions wynd
did driue theyr fhip from that
Iland , fo that they could not
performe their wicked in-
tent. In this his nauigation
our Lord appeared vnto him
many tymes , comforting, &
cherifhing him with incre-
dible confolations, and fpirituall ioyes , and finally he
brought him fafely to the hauen of Ioppa the laft day of
Auguft , and vpon the 4. of
September before noone, to
Hierufalem .

9. It cannot be explica-
ted in few words , what ioy
our Lord imparted to this our
Pilgrim , with the only fight
of that holy Citty, and what

He vifi-
teth the
Holy
places
with ex-
traordi-
nary de-
uotion.

fauour

fauours he did him al the tyme
of his abode there, with a continuall confolation, whilft he
imployed himfelfe in vifiting,
and reuerencing all thofe fa-
cred places, which Chrift our
Lord had fanctified with his
prefence, and delighting exceedingly with the remem-
brance of fo ineftimable a benefit. Our Pilgrim had determined to remayne in Hierufalem, and to imploy the reft
of his life in this holy exercife,
as likewife in affifting, and
feruing his neighbours in all
that his forces could affoard;
though he difcouered not this
laft of helping others, to any,
fearing popular applaufe, and
the good reputatiõ, in which
fome perhaps might haue of
him.

him . But imparting the intention which he had to remayne in Hierusalem , to the
Father Prouinciall of S.Fran-
cis his order who liued there,
and he finding many difficulties and inconueniences therin , following his counsaile,
and the will of God, who called him for greater matters ,
he resolued to returne to
Spayne, & to take that estate,
and manner of life , which
our Lord should vouchsafe to
shew him .

10.   But before his departure from Hierusalem he had
an inflamed desyre to returne,
and visit Mount Oliuet, wher
vntill this day are seene in a
stone the steps which our Sauiour left imprinted with his

What
happe-
ned vn-
to him
vpõ the
Mount
Oliuet .

Diuine

Diuine feet, at the tyme of his
afcending into Heauen : and
with this defyrehe ftole fecre-
tly from the other pilgrims, &
alone without guid, or company , or any Turk to defend
him (which is a very dangerous thing)he went in all haft
vp to Mount Oliuet, & afterward returned to it againe ,ful
of incomparable ioy , that
he might more attentiuely
confider, on what fyde the
ftep of he right , and of the
left foote were placed, which
remayned imprinted in the
ftone. And becaufe he had nothing els to giue to the watch
men , that they would let him
paffe , he gaue them a little
knife , and a payr of fizers
which he had caryed with

him

him. And although the Fathers of S. Francis order, fearing his danger, reprehended him for it, and one of the Christians, who had care of the pilgryms, and was sent for him did both chide, & threaten him, yet our Ignatius was not moued or troubled, for Christ our Sauiour appeared vnto him, and went before him, & bare him company vntill they came to the gates of the Couent: and with this celestiall fauour he endured this trouble with great comfort

Christ our Lord appeareth vnto him.

H 3w

How he returned from Hierusa-
lem into Spaine: and of the
many dangers that
he escaped.

CHAP. V.

THE tyme in which our
Pilgrim returned from
Hierusalé into Italy was very
troublesome with snow, and
frost, being in the hart of
winter. His garment was of
course canuas, and his doublet
which giuen him of almes, was
all cut, and open in the back:
his cloake was short, and thrid
bare, and of bad cloth: he had
no stockings at all, but only
shoes vpon his feet. He found
in Cyprus three ships ready

to depart : one wherof belonged to the Turke , another
which was very ftrong , and
wel appointed was of Venice:
and the third was a little old
bark, almoft rotten and con-
fumed . In this third , our
Ignatius fhipped himfelf , for
the Captayne of the Venetian
fhip vnderftanding that he
was poore, and had not where
withall to pay him , would not
admit him : faying , that if he
were as Holy , as fome gaue
out , he might walk vpon the
water , for he fhould not be
drowned. All thefe three fhips
put themfelues to fayle the
fame day and houre with pro-
fperous wynd ; but in the eue-
ning there came vpon them
a tempeftuous ftorme , with

He re-
turneth
into Ita-
ly and
the little
fhip in
which he
fayling
cometh
home
fafe the
other
being
loft.

E   which

which the Turkish ship was
cast away with all her people:
that of Venice ran herself vpō
ground neere to the Isle of
Cyprus, and was cast away,
though the men in her were
saued: and only the little bark,
in which the seruant of God
went, being old, and worme-
eaten, arriued safe at Venice,
in the middest of Ianuary the
yeare 1524.

2. In Venice he rested himselfe a few dayes, and afterwards tooke his iourney for
Spayn, hauing only 7. or 8.
shillings, which were giuen
him of almes, and a peece of
cloth to couer, and keep warm
his stomack, which he felt to
be much weakened, and consumed by the force of the cold

and

and his nakednes . But going
forward in his iourney , and
being at Ferrara praying in a
Church , there came certaine
poore people to aske of him
almes , and he gaue them all
the money he had , and going
out of the Church, went from
dore to dore asking a peece of
bread to eat according to his
cuſtome .

3. From thence he tooke
his way for Genua, and paſſed
by the armyes , and camps of
the Spaniſh , and French ſouldiers who at that tyme were
at cruell War in Lombardy: &
he was taken for a ſpy & vſed
by the Spaniſh ſouldiers with
little courteſy and modeſty :
for they accouted him a foole,
beating him with their fiſts ,

E 2 　　　　and

and spurning him ; all which
caused extraordinary comfort
in his soule . The French men
vsed him more friendly . And
finally our Lord guiding him
he came to Genua , where he
tooke ship , and with great
danger of Pirats, and enemyes
arriued at Barcelona , ending
his nauigation in the same
place, where he had begun it .

He beginneth to study, to the end
he might help his Neighbours :
And how his life , manners ,
& learning is seuerely ex-
amined , and found
sound & holy.

CHAP   VI.

THE Blessed Father being
returned to Spayne, was

very

very defyrous to pleafe God
and ferue him in whatfoe-
uer he would appoint, but
alwayes with intention to imploy himfelf in helping of his
neighbors. To this end after
he had confidered , and commended the matter much to
God , he refolued to ftudy ,
and to ioyne with the vnction
of Spirit which our Lord imparted vnto him, the ftudy,
and exercife of learning : and
fo he did. And being now 33.
years of age he began to learne
the firft principles of Grammer of a vertuous, and deuout
Maifter called Hierome Arde-
balus , who taught Schoole in
Barcelona , the Lady Elizabeth Rofell (of whom we
fpake before) giuing him all

He be-
ginneth
to ftudy
Grámer.

E 3   that

that was neceſſary for his ſu-
ſtenance ; ſo great was the
ſpirit & feruour with which
he deſyred to ouercome himſelf & pleaſe God .And though
the Diuell tooke vpon him
diuers formes , and vſed new
crafts & deceipts to withdraw
him from his ſtudy : yet the
grace of our Lord , and the
perſeuerance which he gaue
to this his Seruant preuayled
more to make him to goe forward in his Holy Purpoſe ,
then al the deuiſes of the Enemy to hinder him .

2. He felt himſelf in Barcelona ſomwhat eaſed of the
payne of his ſtomack ; and he
preſently returned to the great
rigour of his accuſtomed pennances, which by reaſon of his

want

want of health, and the labour
of so long a iourney, he had
somewhat remitted . Wherefore he made certaine holes in
the soles of his shoes, and tore
them by litle and litle, so that
in the beginning of winter
he went barefoote vpon the
ground, though his feet were
couered with the vpper lea-
thers: & this to auoid ostenta-
tion, which he also did in his
other Pennances .

3. In Barcelona there
befell him two notable thinges
in which he shewed his patience, and charity : The one
was, that hauing notice of
certayne light young men,
who disquieted the Nunnery
called *Of the Angells*, wherein
there liued Religious women

He is misused for the defence of Gods honour.

E 4 of

of S. Dominicks order, & was
scituated at that tyme without
the walls of the citty: he procured to perswade the Nunns
to auoid those conuersations
& occasions, and to giue themselues to all recollection, and
deuotion. By which exhorta-
tions those good fellowes, not
finding their former inter-
taynment in that Monastery,
were much troubled, and
threatned the Blessed Father.
And finally diuers tymes they
refrayned not from blowes,
& once they misused him very
much, so that he had necessity
to be cured: but for all this he
gaue not ouer his enterprize,
reioycing greatly to suffer for
the loue of Iesus Christ.

4.   The second thing was,

that comming one day from
the forefaid monaftery *Of the
Angells* , it happened that a
man had hanged himfelfe v-
pon one of the beames in his
chamber , into which the
good Father fpeedily entred,
and cut downe the rope ; and
though all held the man for
dead , yet did he fall to his
prayers, and cryed vnto him ,
fo that the man recouered his
fenfes, and gaue fignes of re-
pentance, and forrow for his
fins,and a little after gaue vp
the ghoft. In which accident
the circumftances that cōcur-
red were fuch,that it was mi
raculous in the whole Citty,
through which it was foone
diuulged. He ftay d in Barcelona two yeares ftudying

He reftoreth life to one that had hanged himfelfe that he might be forry for his finnes.

Grammer, vntill that by the counsail of some learned men in the yeare 1526. he went to the Vniuersity of Alcala, that he might passe to other higher sciences.

5. In Alcala he lyed in the Hospitall of Lewis of Antezana, which was there founded: & he began to study Logick, and Philosophy: and withall heard the Maister of Sentences, by the counsell of some, who with a desire to haue him end quickly, knew not how to direct him. But he became now so inflamed with the loue of God, & with an insatiable thirst to helpe, and remedy the soules, and bodies of his neyghbours, that he contented not himselfe

with

with the ordinary labour of his ſtudies, and of asking almes from dore to dore, to ſuſtayne himſelfe, but that withall he taught children, and ignorant people the Catechiſme, or Chriſtian Doctrine, and guided many in the way of vertue by prayer, and meditation, and gathered almes with which he prouided victualls for ſuch poore, as ſuffered moſt neceſſity.

6. This cauſed great admiration in that Vniuerſity, and it was more increaſed by ſeing our Bleſſed Father clad with one only coate of courſe cloth, going barefoot, and in his company other three in the ſame attyre, who followed him, as moued by his example;

ample; and besides another
young man of France adioyned himselfe vnto them: So
that they were called (as it
were in mockery) thofe of
the Blancket, or courfe cloth.
This admiration (caufed by
the nouelty) gaue occafion ,
that he and thofe in his company were diuerfly fpoken of
in the towne, euery one inter-
preting that which he did fee,
or heare , according to his
owne affectiō. And although
great diligence, and much
inquiry was made, & diuers
and exquifite informations
taken by the Licenciate Iohn
Figueroa (who afterward
dyed Prefident of Caftilla, &
at that tyme was Vicar Generall of Alcala to the Arch-Bi-

shop

shop of Toledo) of his life, and doctrine : yet there was neuer found in word or deed, any vice in his life, or errour in his doctrine, as the same Vicar testified . Albeit for the greater tryall of the Blessed Father, and that the truth might be more knowe, they afterward apprehended him vpon a false suspition, and kept him in prison 42. dayes with great ioy of his spirit, to see himselfe suffer without fault for Christ, which was the thing that he desired much .

7 . Wherfore though some persons of great Authority who were much deuoted to him, offered him their fauour saying, that they would cause

him

He is cõmitted to prison without any fault.

him to be set at liberty, if he
would; yet he neuer gaue his
consent, nor would take any
Proctor, or Aduocate, nor
any other to plead for his innocency, thinking defence
not to be necessary, where
there was no fault. And likewise if he had done amisse in
any thing, he desired to be
corrected by the Ecclesiasti-
cal Superiors, to whom all his
life he shewed himselfe a child
of obedience. After 42. dayes
the matter being tryed, and
the Processe being concluded, they restored him, and
his company to their former
freedome, the Vicar aforesaid declaring by his sentence
that they were found altogeather innocent, and without

fault

fault in any thing which was obiected againſt them .

8. There happened one thing to the bleſſed Father here in Alcala which was accounted miraculous, and this it was: that the Vicar hauing commaunded when he deliuered him out of priſon, that he ſhould go apparreled like other ſchollers , he commended the matter to a Prieſt named Iohn of Lucena , who imployed himſelfe in workes of charity , deſiring him to procure ſome almes , to buy him cloathes. They two went one day asking this almes, & they came to a ſtreet where many of good ſort ſtood looking on thoſe who were playing at bal, nigh to the houſe of

a prin-

Aknight is conſumed by fyrewho ſaid, that Ignatius ſerued a fagot .

a principall Knight, whom I
wil not name for iust respects.
This Knight vnderstanding
that they asked almes for that
effect, in a great rage, turning to the said Iohn of Lucena, asked him, Why one of
his quality would procure
that almes? And he added,
Let me be burnt, if this fellow de-
erue not to be burned. Which
words were cause of great
scandall to those, who after
came to know it, and were
acquainted with the Fathers
sinctity. But the same day,
there came newes, that King
Philip the second was borne,
in ioy whereof there were
great feasts, and triumphs
made in Alcala, and throughout all Spaine. Vpon which

occasion

occasion the forefaid Knight
went vp to a Turret in his
houfe, where ther was a great
quantity of gun-powder placed, to make artificiall fyers,
and by chance a fparke fell
into the powder, which prefently blew vp the Tower, the
Knight being therwith killed
and burnt.

9. When the bleffed Fa-
ther was told of this, fheding
many teares of pitty, and
compaffion, he fayd: He foretold it himfelfe this morning,
when I paffed by his houfe,
for I wifhed him no fuch
harme. This accident was
very publick, and notorious
in Alcala, and accounted rare,
and miraculous, for the decla-
ration of the Fathers fanctity.

F 10. From

10. From Alcala he went
to speake with Don Alfonsus
of Fonseca Arch-bishop of
Toledo, who at that tyme was
at Valliadolid, and he inter-
tayned him with great benignity, offering him his fauour
and protection, if he would
vse the helpe of him, or his in
Salamanca, giuing him mo-
ney to carry him thither.
When he came thither he began to imploy himselfe (as he
was wont) in stirring vp the
peoples harts to the holy ioue,
and feare of our Lord: In so
much, that within a few
dayes, some Religious, and
zealous persons, moued with
the danger of the tymes, and
the freedome wherwith he
spake, and the concourse of

the

the people who heard him,
(fearing leaſt vnder the
cloke of holynes , ſome euill
might lie hidden which afterward could not be ſo eaſely
remedied) gaue aduiſe to the
Biſhops Prouiſor, and procured that he , and one in his
company ſhould be appre-
hended and caſt into priſon,
being locked togeather ſo
ſtraitly in a great and long
chaine , that they could not
go one from the other, vpō a
ny occaſiō whatſoeuer. But in
that very place the B Father,
omitted not his accuſtomed
exerciſes, nor to ſpeake freely
in the commendation of vertue and reprehenſion of vice,
exciting mens harts to deſpiſe
the world .

How &
why he
was ap-
prehen-
ded in
Sala-
manca.

11. The concourse of people which went to heare him was great, as likewise the fruit which proceeded from his words ; but the ioy of his hart was far greater, to fee himfelfe in fetters, & chaines for Chrift. For all his defires, and wifhes were to dye for our Lord, who dyed for him vpon the Croffe; and fo he tould to fome, who went to comfort him, and fhewed much griefe for his fufferings, reprehending this their falfe pitty and compaffion, becaufe they knew not the treafures, which are contayned in the Croffe of Chrift. They remayned in prifon 22. dayes, receauing many fauours of our Lord in their foules, and

were

were well prouided of all that was necessary for their bodies, by the charity of such deuout persons, as had taken notice of them, and bare them affection. At the end of these 22. dayes, the forsayd Prouisor with the aduise, and consent of other learned men set them at liberty, declaring them to be men of pure and sincere life, & that he had not found any spot, or suspition at all in them.

How he went to Paris to finish his studies. And what happened vnto him there.

CHAP. VII.

IT was Gods will, that this Blessed man should be Fa-

F 3   ther

ther of many children, & therfore, though with contrary
wynds, and boysterous wa-
ues, he guided him to that hauen where he might serue him
according to that which he
himselfe had decreed. To this
end, he gaue him a great, and
inflamed desire, to draw others
into his company, and to imploy himself wholy with them
in the spirituall help of his
neighbours: and withall he
moued him, to go to the Vniuersity of Paris; which at that
tyme was the Mother of all
Vniuersities, & the common
Schoole, and Theater of the
world.

2. The motion, and in-
clination which he had to this
iourney, was with so great

force

force & vehemency, that many spirituall men, and his best friends could not diuert him from it, by propofing vnto him the sharpnes of the tyme, and hard winter, & the open and bloudy war which was betwixt Spayne and France, togeather with the many dangers by the way, alleadging vnto him many, and late examples of horrible crueltyes, which the fouldyers had practifed againft thofe, that trauailed in thofe parts. But all thefe thinges were not fufficient to ftay him, becaufe he felt himfelf caryed with the fauourable wynd of the Holy Ghoft, fynding peace in war, in dangers fecurity, and reft in labours. And fo he tooke his

He goeth to Paris in a cold feafon, & with danger.

iourney through France on
foot, and with the fauour of
God, who guided him, arriued safe at Paris, without paf-
sing any danger, in the beginning of February 1528.

3   At Paris before he went
forward in other higher ftudyes, he perfected himfelfe in
the Latin tongue, ftudying
Humanity almoft two yeares.
After this he began his courfe
of Philofophy, and ended it
with great commendation,
taking the degree of Maifter
of Arts, by his Maifters per-
fuafion, and that by this degre
he might (before men) haue
fome teftimony of his learning, the better to help others.
Hauing ended his courfe of
Philofophy; he ftudyed Di-

His ftu-
dyes, la-
bours &
perfecu-
tions at
Paris.

uinity, our Lord doing him
great mercy, and fauours: and
befydes the labour which he
tooke in ftudying, he endured
other great, & extraordinary
incommodityes For in the beginning he liued in the Hofpitall of S. Iames, asking from
dore to dore that which he
was euery day to eat, and he
was alfo inforced the 3. firſt
yeares to go diuers tymes to
Flaunders, and once into En-
gland to gather fome almes of
the Spanifh merchants (who
refided there) with which he
might poorely fuftayne his
life. He gaue himfelfe likewife
to very auftere pennances, &
to fuch a rigorous life, that it
alone was fufficient to bereaue him of his health, as in

F 5   effect

effect it did, in such sort, that he was constrayned (not without euident perill of his life) to interrupt the course of his studies.

4. Now what shall I say of his other imployments in helping, inflaming, and directing his neighbours to all vertue? What of the most grieuous persecutions which he endured for this cause, which were many, and very continuall? For certaine young schollers, being noble and of excellent witts, hauing forsaken al that they had, to follow the counsailes of Christ our Lord, and moued with the wordes and example of this Blessed Father, made a great change in their life, and gaue

all

all their wealth to the poore ,
begging themſelues from dore
to dore , and lyuing as poore
people in the hoſpitall . This
cauſed a great ſtyrre in the
Vniuerſity , and their kindred
& friends (who were not pleaſed with ſuch courſes) concea-
ued great hatred againſt him ,
whome they knew to be the
author of that new life , which
they accounted folly . And ſo
they began to perſecute , and
calumniate him , raiſing many
falſe teſtimonies againſt him ,
as the world is wont to do , a-
gainſt Gods ſeruants .

    5 . Neither did the mat-
ter end in words alone : for
in the Colledge of S. Barbara ,
where at that time , he ſtudyed
Philoſophy , they would haue

cor-

corrected him publickly, with a feuere, & publick kind of punishment which vfed to be inflicted vpon fuch as were vnquiet, and of a turbulent behauiour: and this, becaufe he exhorted his fchole-fellowes to the deuout frequentation of the Holy Sacraments, and to giue themfelues vpon feftiuall dayes, more then at other tymes, to prayer: and becaufe by this his counfail, a certaine Spanifh fchollar, named Amadore, had left the Colledge, & the world to follow Chrift naked vpon the Croffe.

6. And although the Father knew before, what was intended, and deuifed againft him, and after that the Colledge gates were fhut, and the

bell

bell rung, and the Maisters
ready with their rods in their
hands to correct him, and all
the schollars gathered together to behould this spectacle,
he remayned so vndaunted,
that he was neither troubled,
nor shewed any weakenes:
yea, leaft the glory of Christ
should be diminished, & Vertue dishonoured, and accounted an ignomy amongst Christians, & those tender plants,
which had begun to florish
should be blasted with that
whirldwind, he spake to the
Rector of the Colledge with
such a maiesty, and freedome
(offering himselfe on the one
syde very prompt, and ioyful
to haue that Sacrifice made of
him; & on the other declaring

the

His for-
titude &
alacrity
in igno-
minies
and in-
iuries,

the harme, which those who
were as yet but beginners, &
tender in vertue, would receaue, if he should be punished, for hauing exhorted them
thereunto.) that the Rector
there befor all those who were
gathered together asked pardon of him, as of a Saynt,
who made no account of his
owne ignominy, but only of
the honour of God, and the
good of his neighbours.

7. Thus this chastisement
was omitted, and Vertue remayned with more reputatió,
and the Holy Father came to
be more known: & the Rector
(who was named Doctor
Iames Gouea, of Portugall, a
learned and pious man,) remayned with such affection to
the

the Father, and for his fake to his children, that in progresse of tyme, he was the principal Author who persuaded the King of Portugall, Don Iohn the third, to send the Fathers of the society of Iesus to the East Indies, who since haue done so much good in those remote, and large Prouinces, conuerting innumerable soules of Infidells, to our Holy Religion: our Lord taking so small and ignominious an occasion, for so great a thing, & so much to his glory.

8. Out of all that which men did against the Blessed Father, God drew profit for the Father himself who endured it, & for those who euery day ioyned themselues vnto

him,

him with defyre to imitate the examples of his vertues ; and they ferued alfo for a greater, and more cleere teftimony of the truth. As it happened here in Paris, where his Aduerfaries not contenting themfelues with the calumniations,& falfe fufpitions which they had raifed againft the Bleffed Father, they denounced him alfo to the Inquifitor, who was a learned, and a graue Deuine, called Maifter Matthew Ory, a Friar of S. Dominicks order. But the Inquifitor remayned fo well fatisfyed with the Fathers life, & learning, that he demaunded of him the booke of Exercifes, which he compofed in Manrefa (as we haue faid) and it

pleafed

pleaſed him ſo much, that with
his leaue he tooke a copy of it
for himſelf:&gaue a teſtimony
by authentical Writing, of the
innocency , and purity which
he had found in his life & behauiour . And afterward in
Rome , in a great ſtorme ,
which was raiſed againſt him,
and againſt thoſe of his company, the ſame Inquiſitor was
one of the witneſſes of the
innocency of Bleſſed Father
Ignatius , and an approuer of
his doctrine, as ſhall be declared hereafter .

　　　　G　　　　　*of*

*Of those that adioyned them-
selues to B. F. Ignatius,
and of their vertuous
imployments .*

CHAP.   VIII.

AND because the Father
had an eye, and desire to
get, and procure Company
which might help, and con-
curre to the saluatiō of soules,
our Lord hauing called him to
this so great an enterprise ; he
was attentiue to nothing more
then to gayne some yong men
of good ability, and laudable
cōuersation, who might haue
the same intention : and so he
gained Peter Faber of Sauoy,
Francis Xauier of Nauar,

James

Iames Laynes of Almacan,
Alfonsus Salmerō of Toledo,
Simon Rodericus of Portugal,
and Nicolas Bobadilla, who
was of a place night to Palen-
tia. After these their came likewise to him other three, who
were Claudius Iaius of Sauoy,
Ioan Codury of the Delphi-
nat, and Paschatius Broüet of
the Prouince of Picardy ; so
that they were in all ten. And
though , they were of so
different Nations, as some of
Spayne, and others of France,
at the tyme that those two
Kingdomes were at such terrible warres, notwithstanding
they were all of one and the
same hart ; and will .

   2 . All these were Maisters of Art, and studied Diui-

nity, and the day of the Af-
fumption of our Bleffed Lady
at a Church not farre from
Paris called *Mons Martyrum*,
after they had confeffed, and
receiued the body of Chrift
our Lord, they made a vow
to leaue, vpon a certaine day
appointed, all that they had,
and to imploy themfelues in
the fpirituall profit of their
neighbours, and to goe in
Pilgrimage to Hierufalem, if
cōming to Venice they might
haue commodity to doe it
within a yeare. And if they
could not goe within that
yeare, or if in going they could
not ftay at Hierufalem, to of-
fer themfelues at the Popes
feet, the Vicegerent of Chrift
our Lord, that his Holynes
might

might freely difpofe of them,
in the feruice of the Church,
and the faluation of foules.

3. This being agreed vpon
among themfelues, Bleffed Ignatius gaue order to the reft
to take their iourney towards
Venice, when their ftudyes
were ended; where he would
expect them, after that he had
byn firft in Spaine, and difpat-
ched there certaine bufineffe
for fome of them, and other
important affaires for the feruice of God, which caufed
him to goe thither. With this
refolution he departed from
Paris, and came to his owne
Countrey, where though his
Brother were Lord of the
Place, yet he would by no
meanes lodge in his houfe,

nor take that , which he
needed of him, but liued in
the hospitall, asking his poore
Victualls from dore to dore.
There he taught the Cate-
chisme, of Christiā Doctrine,
and preached with such concourse of people which came
from many villages , that he
was inforced to preach in the
fields , because the multitude
could not be contayned in the
Churches , and many that
they might heare, and see him
the better , climbed vp into
trees : and though the Father
was very weake, and sicke of
an ague, yet he preached thrice
euery weeke ; and all the
words which he spake , were
plainely heard more then a
quarter of a mile, from the

place

place wherin he stood, which
semed very strange, and miraculous.

4. With these his Sermons
he rooted out many vices, and
established many things profitable for sustayning the poore,
and the amendment of those
who were in mortall sin, prouiding in all things for the
good both of soules & bodyes,
and leauing all that Country
in admiration, and replenished
with a most sweet odour of his
vertues, and the miracles
which God wrought by him.
For in that place he healed a
man named Vastida, who had
byn many yeares much troubled with the gout; and a vertuous woman who had byn in
a cōsumption for some space;

He cu-
reth a
man
of the
gout, &
a womā
in a con-
sumptiō
and ano
ther pos-
sessed.

G 4   and

and deliuered another, who had byn tormented by the Diuell foure yeares. And our Lord wrought other things by his meanes, which were held for miraculous; by reason wherof, and for his holy life, all the people respected him so much, that they did striue to touch his garments, esteming him as a Saint, and a great Seruant of God.

5. From hence alone, & without money, asking almes by the way, he went to Pampelona, and from thence to Almacan, Siguença, & Toledo, to dispatch the busines which was commended vnto him. Afterward he took ship, neere to Valentia, for Italy, and with great labour, incom-

modityes and dangers, he arriued with our Lords fauour
at Venice, to expect his company there, as they had agreed
in Paris. But the Diuell efte-
ming him now his open enemy, and forefeeing the warre
which he was to make againft
him, did perfecute him there
alfo, and by certayne of his
minifters publifhed, that he
was a fugitiue, and that his
ftatua being burnt, was fled
from Spayne, and other things
of like nature, but all falfe;
and were declared to be fuch
by Hierome Verall Archbi-
fhop of Rofa, who after was
Cardinall of the Church of
Rome, and at that tyme Apoftolicall Nuncius in Venice.
In the tyme that he ftayed for

He is ac-
cufed at
Venice
and de-
clared
innocêt.

G 5   his

his company he did much
good, drawing many learned,
& pious men to Gods feruice,
who vnited themfelues with
him, and directing fome of
thofe Senators to all vertue,
and leauing a moft fweet memory of himfelfe, with all that
knew, and conuerfed with
him.

6.　His. company came
from Paris to Venice the 8. of
Ianuary 1537. hauing endured much by the way, it being
long, and the tyme fharp, and
rigorous, and they comming
alfo on foot with much dif-
commodity : but they ouercame all difficultyes by the
particuler graces, which God
gaue them, and with an inflamed defire to fuffer much for

him

The reft
of his
compa-
ny com-
meth to
Venice,
& there
ferue in
the hof-
pitalls.

him. In Venice they found their Father, and Maifter Ignatius, with the other cõpany which was come vnto him, and they imbraced on another with exceding great contentment. They prefently deuided themfelues into diuers Hofpitalls, to ferue and affift the poore. Afterward they went to Rome on foot, with extreme pouerty, and need, afking almes, and fafting euery day, becaufe it was in Lent: where hauing receiued the benediction of Pope Paul the 3. to goe to Hierufalem with the fame pouerty, they returned to Venice, where Father Ignatius remayned.

7. There thofe who were not priefts tooke that order,

the

They are
made
Priests
& deui-
de them-
selues in
the state
of Ve-
nice.

the day of S. Iohn Bapt. in the
same yeare 1537. hauing before
made the vowes of Chastity,
and Pouerty, in presence of
the Apostolicall Legate. And
to expect their going to Hierusalem, they deuided themselues
in the Citties of the dominion
of Venice: and Fa. Ignatius,
with Father Faber, & Father
Laynes remayned 40. dayes
without the Citty of Vincenza, in a little house, or Hermi-
tage, which was left desolate
& halfe falne downe, without
dores, or windowes, so that
the wind, and water entred
in on all sides. They slept
on the ground vpon a little
straw, and had nothing to eat,
but a few hard, and mouldy
crusts of bread, which were

giuen

giuen them of almes, not with
out difficulty , feething them
firft in a little water, that they
might be able to eat them.

8 . But afterward hauing
wholy loft their hope of going
to Hierufalem , they refolued
to deuide themfelues in the
chiefe Vniuerfities of Italy :
& B. F. Ignatius with Father
Faber and F. Laynes went to
Rome , whither God called
them , to begin the new Society, & Order , which through
the whole world, was fo much
to increafe his glory . It was
a very markeable thing that
for many yeares before that of
1537. & after that vntil 1570.
there neuer fayled fome fhips
for pilgrims to go to Hierufalem , but only that yeare . For

our

our Lord directed the courses
of this Blessed Father , and
of these in his company for
higher matters, then they vnderstood , or thought of in the
beginning.

*The Society of Iesus is founded,
and confirmed by the Sea A-
postolick: and Ignatius
is ordained Generall.*

CHAP. IX.

THE Blessed Father, after
he was made Priest , had
take a whole yeare to prepare
himselfe for his first Masse. In
this tyme. he imploied himselt
with all the forces of his soule
most humbly beseeching the
glorious Virgin Mary, the Mo

*Ignatius
his de-
uotion
to our B·
Lady.*

ther

ther of God, that shee would bring him vnto her Sonne: & that since she is the Gate of Heauen, and a singular Aduocate betwixt God and Man, she would procure him entrance, that her most Blessed Sonne might take notice of him by her meanes, and he might come to knowe her Sonne, & reuerēce him with a most entire hart & deuotion. He added moreouer, that since the enterprise, which he had vndertaken for his seruice, was so great and hard, that shee would open the gate, and take away the difficulties which might hinder in so important an affaire.

2. With these desyres, & wishes the B. Father tooke

his

his way towards Rome, on foot, with F. Faber, and F. Laynes in his cōpany, asking almes, as they were wont : and he receiued the moſt Sacred Body of our Lord euery day at their hands : and in all his iourney, he was illuſtrated, and ſtrengthned with heauen-ly inſpirations, and ſpirituall comforts. But one day dra-wing nigh to the Citty of Rome, leauing the two Fa-thers in the field, he went into a deſert, and ſolitary Church ſome mile from the Citty to pray. There amidſt the grea-teſt feruour of his prayers, he felt his hart changed, and God the Father appeared to him, together with his moſt Bleſſed Sonne, who carried

the

the Croſſe vpon his ſhoulders:
and with the eyes of his ſoule,
illuſtrated with that reſplen-
dent light, he ſaw that the E-
ternall Father, turning to his
only begotten Sonne, com-
mended Ignatius, and thoſe in
his company vnto him, with
exceeding great loue, putting
them into his hands. And our
moſt benigne Ieſus hauing receiued thē vnder his patrona-
ge, & protectiō, as he ſtood in
that manner, with his Croſſe,
turned to Ignatius, and with a
louing, and mild countenance
ſaid vnto him: *Ego vobis Romæ
propitius ero:* I will be fauourable to you at Rome.

3. With this diuine reue-
lation, our Father remayned
very much comforted, and

Chriſt
with his
Croſſe
appea-
reth to
him and
promi-
ſeth hir
his fa-
uour.

H   ſtrength

strengthned , and he related it afterwards to thofe in his cō-pany , to animate them the more, and to prepare them for the troubles which they were to endure : And with this vifi-on, together with many other excellent illuftrations which he had , the moft Sacred name of IESVS, was fo imprinted in his foule, with an earneft de-fyre to take our Sauiour for his Captaine, carrying his Croffe after him ; that this was the caufe, that at his , and the other firft Fathers humble fuite , and requeft , the Apo-ftolicke Sea, at the Confirma-tion of our Religion, called, & named it, THE SOCIETIE OF IESVS; which was firft done by Pope Paul the

third,

Why he called his order the Society of Iesvs.

third of that name, after a terrible tempest, which was raised against it in Rome, by occasion of a certaine hereticall Preacher, to whome our Fathers opposed themselues. Which storme soon ceased, by reason that our Lord brought in that occasion, and in that very tyme, not without a singular & particuler prouidence, those who had been the Blessed Fathers Iudges in Spayne, France, and Venice, that now they might be witnesses of his innocency, and vertue. By which meanes the truth being knowne, the Gouernour of Rome, pronounced sentece in fauour of our Blessed Father, and of those in his company, by order of his Holynes.

4. Who

What difficulty there was in the confirmatiō of the society.

4. Who to proceed more maturely in the busines of the Confirmatiō of this Religion, committed it to three Cardinalls, who in the beginning were very opposite & auerred, especially Cardinall Bartholo. mæus Guidichion, because he iudged, that new Orders of Religion were not fit to be begun, but the ancient reformed, according to the Decree of Innocentius the third in the Lateran Councell, & of Gregory the tenth in the Councell of Lyons. Which very difficulty, those two great, and glorious Patriarks S. Dominick and S. Francis had in the Confirmation of their Sacred Religions: for the workes of God must passe through this

examine

examine, and fornace.

5. But our Lord Iesus hauing now taken Ignatius vnder his wings, and promised to fauour him in Rome, changed the mind of Cardinall Guidichion in such sort, that he was heard to vtter these words: *I like not new Religions but yet I dare not omit to approue this: for I feele inwardly in my hart such extraordinary motions, that the diuine Will carryeth me to that, which I am not inclined to by reason; and imbrace that with my affection, which by the force of humane reasons I vtterly disliked.* And thus this very Cardinall commended the Institute of the Society very earnestly to the Pope: & his Holynes read it, and with the spi-

rit

rit of the Chiefe Bishop said:
Digitus Dei est hic : This is the
finger of God; affirming, that
from so smal, and weak beginnings he hoped for, and expected no small fruit for the
Church of God. And so he
confirmed the Religion of the
Society, in the yeare 1540. the
27. of September, which is
the feast of the S. Cosmus &
Damianus: but yet he added a
certaine Limitation, which he
tooke away three yeares after,
cōfirming the Society a new.
And the yeare 1550. Pope Iulius the third, who succeeded
Pope Paul, approued it againe:
and the other Popes, who haue
followed since, haue established, & enriched it with many
Graces, & priuiledges, as may

be

Pope
Paul the
the third
confir-
meth the
Society.

be seene in their Bulles, and in
the Summary therof.

6. But returning to our
blessed Father Ignatius, when
the Society was thus confirmed, by the Vicegerent of
Christ (as we haue said) there
met in Rome, the Lent following in the yeare 1541. the
first Fathers who remayned
in Italy, for the election of a
Generall, and the others sent
their suffrages by writing.
And by common consent of
all, the B. Father was declared Generall. His humility
was so great, that he could
not possibly be perswaded to
accept of it, but intreated the
Fathers most effectuously not
to giue him that charge, of
which he was so vnworthy,

He is
made
General.

H 4   and

and which he could not exer-
cise without the domage, and
harme of the Society . So that
finally they were inforced to
comfort him , and to con-
descend to him so farre , as to
take other foure dayes to
commend that affayre to our
Lord anew , and to beseech
him to discouer vnto them his
holy will . But they continued in their former resolution the second time also,
which notwithstanding was
not sufficient to ouercome
the Fathers humility, and the
true contempt which he had
of himselfe, vntill being re-
tired for some dayes, and hauing made a generall Con-
fession in S. Peters *de Monte
aureo,* to a Father of S. Francis

Order

Order, called Fryar Theophilus, a holy man, and of great parts (with whom before the confirmation of the Society, he was wont to confesse) he tould him , that he refisted the holy Ghost , in resisting his Election.

7. To this voyce our humble Father Ignatius yeilded himselfe , bowing his neck to the yoke , which our Lord laid vpon him : and the 22. day of Aprill of the same yeare 1541. he went with the other Fathers, and three Brothers (of which my selfe was one) to visit the 7. Churches and Stations of Rome, and in the Church of S. Paul he said masse, and made his profession, giuing the B. Sacra-

H 5   ment

ment to the other Fathers, who likewise made their profession in his hands, shedding many teares, for their spirituall ioy, and feruent deuotion: Yeelding many thanks to our Lord, becaufe he had vouchfafed to bring that to effect, and finall perfection, which himfelfe had begun. From that day forward the Society was acknowldged, for a Religion approued by the Sea Apoftolike, hauing in it Religious men obliged with their folemne vowes, and profeffion, and with a Superiour and head, who was to gouerne it for Gods greater glory, and the good of his Church.

How

How he behaued himselfe being
made Generall; & of diuers
new Colledges founded
by his meanes.

CHAP. X.

PRESENTLY after he
was made Generall, the
first thing that he did, was to
rise very early the next morning, and to awake all the
house; iudging it to be his office to watch prepetually ouer
all, and to procure, that all his
subiects should watch, & euery
one attend carefully to their
imployment. And to humble,
and debase himselfe so much
the more, by how much the
degree in which God had pla-

ced

ced him was high and emi-
nent, he went into the kit
chin, and performed the office of Cooke, and such other
things of like quality for ma
ny dayes, with such diligence
that he seemed a Nouice, who
did it only for his owne greater profit, and mortification.

2. This being ended he
began to catechize, or teach
the Christian Doctrine in our
Church, which he continued
for the space of six, and forty
dayes, explicating daily the
commandements, articles, &
other things appertayning to
the principles of our holy
faith. All which he declared
in Italian, with improper,
and vnpolished words, but
vttered with such spirit, and

force, that they moued the
hearers to compunction; in
such sort, that they were so
pierced with sorrow, that
presently vpon hearing him
they went to confession, and
could scarce speake by reason
of the aboundance of teares
and sighes, with which they
bewayled their sinnes. Of
which I my selfe am witnes,
being at that tyme but very
young, and repeating euery
day that which the B. Father
had taught.

3. Besides all this, the holy
Father attended to plant, pro-
pagate, and extend his new
order of religion throughout
the world. He sustayned it
with his prayers, ruled it with
his wisedome, gaue it life

with

with his spirit, defended it with his valour, and edified, and inflamed it to all vertue with his example. And our Lord, who had chosen, and preuented him with the blessings of his sweetnes, fauoured him with so large a hand, that whatsoeuer the B. Father vndertooke, seemed prosperous and secure. In so much, that after the Society was confirmed by the Sea Apostolike, (they at that tyme being so few) our Lord spread them in such sort ouer the world, that within the space of one yeare, they were in France, Italy, Germany, Spayne, Portugall, Ireland, and the West Indies, not without much admiration.

The propagation of the Society within a yeare after the confirmation.

4. Our

4. Our B. Father was Ge-
nerall for the space of fifteene
yeares, three moneths, and
nine dayes, from the 22. of
Aprill, in the yeare of our
Lord 1541. vntill the laſt of
Iuly 1556. in which he departed this world. All this
tyme he remayned in Rome,
without going thence, vnles
it were twiſe, once into the
Kingdome of Naples, and another tyme to the Citty of
Oruieto, where Pope Paul
the third was at that ſeaſon;
both which iourneis he vndertooke for affayres of great
importance.

5. In all theſe yeares his
imployments were to found,
and gouerne by himſelfe, the
houſe of Rome (which is the

The B.
Fathers
employ-
ments
being
General.

mother

mother, and Head of the rest)
and to send his children to
preach in the world, giuing
them instructions, by obser-
uation wherof they might become worthy workemen of
Iesus Christ; who with the
edification, which by Gods
fauour they caused in all
parts, drew the peoples affection vnto them, & increased
their deuotion in such sort,
that many desired Colledges
of the Society to the end they
might receiue the more profit
by their doctrine, and holy in-
stitution. And to this the
holy Father did carefully coo-
perate, sending those of the
Society to the places, which
seemed most necessary, and
conuenient for the founda-

tion

tion of such Colledges, and houses, as were required: and that this plant, which our Lord of his goodnes would haue to increase so much in his Church, might dayly be more firmely rooted.

6. And because the Diuell bare great hatred, and enuy to the B. Father, and his religion, and in all parts moued great contradictions and persecutions against it; he as a valiant Captaine encountred the common enemy, making as fierce resistance against him, and clearing the truth, not permitting that such lyes, as the Diuell by his ministers spread abroad should preuaile against it. Notwithstanding the Father was not content

I with

with these so many, & so great
imploymēts, which had beene
able to weary a Gyant : but
with an enflamed desire, and
charity to helpe his neighbours (as if he had nothing
els to do) he laboured to profit them abroad , and procured to extirpate certayne vices
out of the Citty of Rome, & to
institute therin many workes
much to Gods glory, and the
spirituall benefit of soules.

7 . As for example: that
the Phisitians should not cure
the bodyes of the sick, before
their soules were cured with
the holy sacrament of Confession, according to the Decre-
tall of Innocentius the third.
That there should be a house
erected in Rome for the *Cathe-*

cumeni

The pi-
ous wor-
kes
which
he did in
Rome.

cumeni , in which the Iewes , and Infidells , who defired baptifme, and are brought to the knowledg of the Truth, might be receyued and maintayned. To him likewife is the worke , commonly knowne by the appellation of *Our Lady of Grace* , to be attributed , which was begunne in the monaftery of S. Martha, wher there was a Confraternity, or brotherhood inftituted to recollect , and retyre all fuch maryed, or vnmaryed womē, as remained in euill eftate, vntill they were reconciled to their husbands, or had fome other condition wherin they might liue without our Lords offence .

8 . And the charity of the

Blessed Father was so great,
that when these poore women
forsooke their euill life, he
himselfe would accompany
them through the Citty, not
withstanding his yeares, authority, or office of Generall.
And whereas some tould him,
that he lost his tyme, because
these women through their
euill custome, did easely returne to their former vices,
the holy man answered with
maruelous repose: *I account not
this labour lost, yea I assure you,
that if with the labours & cares of
my whole life, I could procure any
one of these to passe only one night
without sinning, I would esteeme
them well bestowed, that the infinite Maiesty of my Creator, and
Lord, might not be offended in*

that

that short space.

9. He laboured no lesse to relieue the necessity, & solitude of Orphanes. And so the two houses which are in Rome, for such children of both sexes were by his meanes erected. Likewise with no lesse, yea with more care, he procured the foundation of the Monastery of S. Catherine in Rome, called *de Funarij*; in which Virgins, who eyther by the negligence or defect of vertue in their mothers, or by reason of their pouerty are in danger, doe retire themselues, as to a sanctuary. For his charity was so great, that he alway treated of such things, as might profit his neighbours, and further their saluation. And that this

I 3 *charity*

charity of the Blessed Father,
togeather with his fortitude,
and constancy, in the workes
which he vndertook for Gods
greater seruice, might the better appeare, our Lord permited
terrible persecutions, and tem-
pests to be raised against him,
for these his good, and profitable labours : which not-
withstading finally did breake
their furious waues vpon the
rocke of truth, and the workes
remained more firme with
these contradictions; and the
Fathers sanctity more approued, and knowne.

10. It cannot easely be be-
lieued, how many things were
borne vp, and sustayned with
the shoulders of this diuine
Giant, and with what valour,

and spirit he sustayned them ,
especially hauing so weake ,
and sickly a body . For besides
the affaires already mentioned
which had byn sufficient to
weary many men, diuers Princes , and persons of all quali-
tyes , did write vnto him ,
from almost all the parts , and
Prouinces of the world. Some
for their deuotion commended themselues to his prayers.
others to benefit themselues
by his prudence and wisdome,
demaundinge his counsell :
others to help themselues with
his fauour, and industry in
dispatching businesse : others
to giue him thankes for the
benefits , and good assistance
receiued from his children :
and others for other respects .

And they were fo many, that only this emploiment had byn fufficient to tyre any ftrong man, if he had not byn vp-holden by the mighty hand of our Lord , who gaue him forces for all . So that when he was moft weary, fickly , and alone , and without the helps which were neceffary for fo great a charge, he feemed moft ftronge ; and in his weaknes was difcouered , and fhined the vertue and force of God.

Of the happy Death of B. Igna-
tius : and what happe-
ned therat .

C H A P.   X I.

THE bleffed Father with the force of his foule fup-

ported

ported the weakenes of his body, enduring with great patience the troubles of this pilgrimage, and conforming himselfe in all things to the will of God: but he had such an enflamed desire to see, and enioy him, that he could not suppresse the gladnes which he coceiued in thinking vpon his passage out of this world, without teares. Wherfore being now loaden with yeares, wearied with sicknes, afflicted with the perturbation, & new calamityes of the Church, and hauing an ardent desire to be with Christ, he began to beseech him with many teares and sighes, that he would vouchsafe to take him out of this exile, and banishment and carry him to that place of rest, where he might praise him, and enioy his blessed presence, with the freedome, which he desired.

2. And our Lord heard his request, giuing him certayne signes, and pledges therof. Whereupon, in a letter which he wrot to Doña Leonora Mascareñas, who had byn Nurse to Phillip the second, the Catholike King of Spayne, and his very deuout daughter, he tooke his leaue of her, telling her (as she her selfe afterward told me) that, thet should be the last letter, which he would write vnto her, & that he would earnestly commend her to God in heauen. Wherefore vnderstan-

ding

He foreknew his death & wrot of it to Doña Leonora Mascareñas.

ding that this fo happy , and
ioyfull a day for him approa-
ched (though at that tyme he
had not any great ficknes, but
only his ordinary weakenes ,
and indifpofition , which feemed not ftrang to them that
lyued with him) the Bleffed
Father went to Confeffion ,
and receiued the bleffed Sacrament , as he was wont to
do , when he could not fay
Maffe : and vpon the 30. day
of Iuly at three of the clocke
in the afternoon, he called for
Father Iohn Polancus Secre-
tary of the Society: who litle
thinking what he would haue
with him, the B Father tould
him with exceding great .e-
pofe , that the houre of his de
parture out of this world drew

neere

neere, willing him prefently
to go kiffe the Popes Holynes
feet in his name, and to craue
his bleffing for him, and a
Plenary Indulgence of his
finnes, that fo he might enter
with more confidence and
comfort into that his laft iourney : all which his Holynes
graunted very willingly, giuing great fignes of loue, and
griefe

3. The Phifitians being
called, faid, that the fickneffe
was not dangerous, and the
Father made no alteration in
his proceeding (for being fo
humble, he would not make
any oftentation of the gifts receiued from our Lord, nor of
that which he knew, but let
the Phifitians do their office,

and

and permitted, that their opinion, and counsell should be taken, and followed in all things:) and in this manner the next morning, which was Friday, one houre after sunne rising, lifting vp his hands, & fixing his eyes on Heauen, calling vpon I E S V S with his toung and hart, with a serene and quiet countenaunce, he rendered his Blessed soule to him, who had created it for his so great Gory, the last of Iuly in the yeare 1556. A man truly humble which he shewed euē in that his last houre: since that knowing (as he did) the tyme of his death, he named no Vicar Generall (as he might haue done) nor would call his children to exhort

them

His departure the last of Iuly. 1556.

them , and to giue them his
Blessing , nor make any other
demonstration of a Father , to
signify that he had done nothing , and accounted himself
as nothing in the foundation
of the Society .

4. He deceased at the age
of threescore and fyue yeares,
and in the 35. yeare after his
Conuersion: in which space
he liued in extreme pouerty,
pennances , peregrinations ,
labours in study, persecutions,
prisons, fetters , with other
great troubles , and molestations, all which he endured
with a cherefull, & admirable
constancy , for the loue of
Iesus Christ , who gaue him
victory ouer the Diuells , & all
his other aduersaryes which
                    procu-

procured to ouerthrow him.
He liued 16. yeares after the
Society was confirmed by the
Sea Apoſtolick, and in them
he ſaw it multiplyed, and extended almoſt thoroughout
the whole world. He left eſta-
bliſhed 12. Prouinces, that of
Portugall, of Caſtilla, of Ara-
gonia, of Andaluzia, of Italy
(which cōprehendeth Lum-
bardy, and Toſcan) of Naples,
of Sicily, of Germany, of
Flaunders, Fraunce, of Bra-
ſile, and of the Eaſt Indies: &
in theſe Prouinces there was
at that tyme about one hundred Colledges, or Houſes of
the Society.

5. The death of ſo Holy
and excellent a man cauſed
great feeling, and ſorrow in

Rome,

Rome, especially amongst his children, who remained there, & afterward in the rest of the Society, in which presetly after his deceale, the fauour which preceded from their dead, or rather truly lyuing Father was perceyued. For throughout the whole Society there ensued a most tender feeling of his most fragrant memory, ioyned with teares of cófort, and a desyre replenished with holy hope, togeather with a certayne vigour, and fortitude of spirit: so that they all seemed to burne with new desyres of labouring, and suffering for Christ.

6. His body was placed in a low, and humble tombe, the first day of August at the

right

right hand of the high Altar, in our litle Church of the B. Virgin Mary in Rome. Afterward vpon the fame day of his death in the yeare 1569. it was trâflated to another place in the fame Church, becaufe the high Altar was changed: and finally in the yeare 1587. vpon the 19. day of Nouember which is dedicated to S. Pontianus Pope, and Martyr, it was tranflated againe, with great folemnity to the new, and fumptuous Church of the Profeffed Houfe, which Cardinall Alexander Farnefius had erected.

7. It was placed in a cheft of lead, vnder a vault, at the right hand of the high Altar, with a playne ftone, which

couereth the graue, and in the
walla black shining marble ,
in which these words are en-
grauen .

D . O . M .

IGNATIO SOCIETATIS IE-
SV FVNDATORI. OBDORMI-
VIT IN DOMINO AETATIS
SVAE ANNO LXV . CONFIR-
MATI A SEDE APOSTOLICA
ORDINIS XVI. SALVTIS HV-
MANAE M.D.LVI. PRID.KAL.
AVG.EIVS IN CHRISTO FILI)
PARENTI OPTIMO POSS.

That is ,

To Ignatius Founder of the
Society of Iesus, as to their
most louing Father his childrē
in Christ erected this memory.
He rested in our Lord in the
55.ye re of his age , and in the
15 .after the Confirmation of

his

his Religion by the Sea Apo-
ftolick, and in the yeare of our
redemption 1556 . the day before the Calends of Auguft.

8. In this place remay-
neth the body of this Bleffed
Patriarch at this day, reuerenced not only by all his childré,
but alfo by the people, and
Court of Rome, & thofe who
repaire thither for their deuo
tion; by reafon of the great o-
pinion, which they haue of
his admirable life, and excel-
ient fanctity: as alfo for the
Miracles, which our Lord
worketh euery day by his interceffion, to exalt him, and
make him glorious in the
world: and by reafon of the
fruit, which they fee brought
forth by the labours, induftry,

K 2   and

and trauaile of his children :
iudging that the roote, which
hath produced such a plant,
could not choose but be exceeding perfect, nor the fountayne but very plentifull, and
acceptable to our Lord, from
which hath flowed so aboundant, and holesome waters of
vertue, and learning, to water
the world, which was before
so dry & barren, and replenished with bryars and thornes.

9. His stature was with the
least: his conntenaunce very
graue: his forehead broad, and
playne : his eyes were somewhat hollow; the lids whereof
were a little wrinckled, &
gathered together by reason of
many teares which he continually shed: his eares of a mid-

dle

dle fiſe : his noſe ſomewhat
high, & lifted vp in the midſt :
his colour though ſallow , yet
liuely, and his head venerably
bald. The máner of his geſture
was cherefully graue, and gra-
uely cherefull : ſo that with his
ſerenity he reioyced thoſe who
beheld him, and with his gra-
uity compoſed them . He hal-
ted a little of one lege , which
was ſomewhat ſhorter then
the other (by reaſon of the
wound, which he receiued, &
the bones, that were taken
out of it) but without defor-
mity ; and with the modera-
tion, which he obſerued in his
gate , it could hardly be perceiued .

K 3   *Of*

*Of the chiefest Vertues of B . Ig-
natius : & especially of his
Humility ,& contempt
of himselfe .*

CHAP. XII.

BVT who can worthily
relate in this place , that
harmony, and comfort of admirable vertues which were
to be seene in the Blessed Father ? Who can discouer the
treasures, and heauenly gifts,
with which God enriched , &
adorned him ? Who is able to
explicate the asperity of his
pennance? the perfectiõ of his
contempt of the world ? his
profound humility? inuincible
patience ? amiable meeknes ?

The
vertues
of the
Holy Fa-
ther.

his

his fo rare fpirituali prudence?
fo fweet, and effectuall gouerment of his fubiects? his forti
tude, and conftancy in aduerfityes, and contradictions? his
confidence, and courage in
vndertaking hard, and difficult attempts for our Lords
loue? his vigilancy, and follicitude in feeing them performed? his burning, and enflamed loue of God, and of his
neighbours? his continuall
prayer with which his foul enioyed the vifitations of her
fweeteft fpoufe? and finally
his miracles, and the wonderfull workes which our Lord
hath done, and dayly doth by
his meanes?

2. For to omit the rigour
of his pennances, his naked-

nes, hunger, and cold, his dif-
ciplines, and hayrclothes, and
all other kynd of penaltyes,
with which he afflicted his
body, from the tyme that he
began to serue our Lord, he
most affectuously imbraced
the vertue of Humility, as the
foundation of all other vertues: going torne, and halfe
naked, and liuing in the Hofpitalls as a poore man, among
other of that quality, despised,
and contemned and desyrous
not to be knowne, or esteemed of any, and very ioyfull
when he was neglected, and
persecuted for the loue of Iesus Christ our Redeemer; by
which he taught vs, that he
who pretendeth to ascend on
high, must begin very low,

and

His hu-
mility.

and that according to the height of the building, the foundation muſt be layd low; and that for the conuerſion of ſoules this affect of true humility helpeth more, then to ſhew authority, which hath ſome taſt, or ſauour of the world.

3. I heard him ſay, that al thoſe of the houſe gaue him example of vertue, and matter of confuſion, and that he was not ſcandalized at any of them, but only at himſelfe. And in a letter, which I haue ſeene, he wrot, that he had neuer treated with any of ſpirituall affayres, how great a ſinner ſoeuer he was, that he ſeemed not to haue gayned much by that communication. Doubtles becauſe he eſteemed

K 5 himſelfe

himselfe a greater sinner. And
to this purpose he was wont
to say, that he did not think,
there was any in the world;
who on the one side receyued so great, and so continuall fauours at Gods hands:
and on the other, was so de
fectiue, and carelesse in his
seruice. One day, as we were
togeather alone, he tould me,
that he was to beseech our
Lord, that his body after his
death might be cast vpon a
dunghill, that it might be eaten by foules, and doggs. *For*
I being (saith he) *as I am, an*
abhominable dunghill, yea very
dung it selfe, what other thing
should I desyre, for the punish-
ment of my synns?

4.   He desyred, that all

should

should ieſt , and mock at him ,
and ſaid, that if he would ſuffer
himſelfe to be caryed away by
his feruour , and deſire , he
ſhould goe vp, and downe the
ſtreets naked, and al bemyred,
that he might be accounted a
foole. But he repreſſed this ſo
great an affect of Humility
with his charity, and deſyre to
helpe his neighbours . Very
ſeldome (and then not without great cauſe)did he ſpeake
of any thing belonging to
himſelfe, and when others did
ſpeake of them in his preſence,
or of any thing els , which
might redound to his prayſe ,
he preſently recollected himſelf , not without teares , and
bluſhing .

5 . The Bleſſed Father

had

had at one tyme for his Confeſſarius an ancient Father of
the Society, of the Kingdome
of Nauar, who was called Dõ
Diego Eguia, ſo perfect, and
holy a man, that our Father
himſelfe ſaid vnto me: when
we ſhalbe in Heauē Don Diego wilbe ſo far eleuated aboue
vs, that we ſhall ſcarſe be able
to ſee him. This Father ſpake
moſt earneſtly of the vertue,
and ſanctity of our B. Father, as
one who knew his conſciēce,
and the purity, and the orna-
ment of his ſoul. The B Father
tooke this very ill, and commaunded him in vertue of holy
obedience, that he ſhould not
ſpeake any word therof ſo
long as he lyued, and not being able to repreſſe him, he left

of

of confeſſing with him. And
the holy ould man was wont
to ſay, that he deſired to liue
ſome dayes after the death of
our Father, that he might declare, what he knew ; but our
Lord ſo ordayned, that he died
three dayes before, and as it
was thought, at the requeſt of
our Bleſſed Father.

6. He arriued by Gods
grace to ſo great, and perfect
a knowledge of himſelfe, that
for many yeares before his
death, he had not any temptation of vayne glory. For his
ſoule was ſo illuſtrated with
light from heauen, that he was
wont to ſay, that he feared no
vice leſſe then vayne glory,
which is a worme, wont to
eat, and conſume the Cedars

of

of Libanus, and is bred by the blynd loue, and estimation of our selues. All that belonged vnto him sauoured of Humility : his apparell was poore though cleanly, his bed poore, his food & sustenance poore, and so sober and temperate, that it was a perpetuall abstinence, being also course, and homely. He imploied himselfe willingly in the most humble offices of the house, and in making of the beds, and dressing vp the chambers of the sicke: and he suffered himselfe to be so easily ruled by the iudgment of others, that though he were Superiour , yet he equalled himselfe in all things to his inferiors : yea he did not only equall, but also submit, and

subiect

ſubiect himſelfe vnto them,
with admirable meekenes, &
humility.

7. In the tyme that he
taught the Catechiſme, or
Chriſtian Doctrine, a boy,
which was in the houſe told
him with great plaineſſe and
ſimplicity, that he ſpake bad
Italian, and that he ſhould do
wel to labour to ſpeak better.
To whom the Father anſwe-
red. *Thou haſt good reaſon, Boy, I*
pray thee note my faultes, and tell
me of them. One of the cauſes
why he deſired to haue his religion called the SOCIETY
OF IESVS, was, not to be
named, and mentionéd him-
ſelfe, and that it might be
thought, that he had no part
in it: and when he ſpake of
it,

it , he alwayes said *this least
Society*: for as he was the least
in his owne eyes, so he would
haue his children to esteeme
themselues such . Now what
shall I say of that Humility ,
with which so earnestly , and
so often he refused to be Generall , and would neuer accept
that Office , vntill his Confessarius charged his côscience
and obliged him therunto ?

8 . Neither was he con-
tent with this , but afterward
also in the yeare 1550 . he caused the grauest Fathers of the
Society to meete in Rome,
that he might resigne his
Charge, protesting before our
Lord, and affirming in a letter,
which he wrote vnto them ,
that he had many, and diuers

tymes ferioufly iudged , that
he wanted in a manner infinite degrees of thofe parts and
talents which were required
in him , who fhould haue that
Charge , and Office. For thefe
were his very wordes : Wheras all wee who were acquainted with him , knew , that he
had fo great , and notable a
gift in gouerning , that all the
excellent Superiours of Religions might take him for a
patterne , and example. And
though he could not obtayne
his defire at this tyme , yet he
omitted not to treat of the
fame renunciation againe ,
that he might retyre himfelfe ,
alwell to giue himfelfe with
more freedome to contempla-
tion , and enioy by folitari-

L   neſſe

nesse, his soueraigne Good, as also because (as he tould me) it seemed to him, that he was good for nothing, and that he hindred some other from gouerning the Society, who might profit it more. But he went not forward with his intentiō at this tyme: for he was told, that the Society would in no sort yield vnto it, nōr consent to haue any other Superiour, so long as it pleased God to prolong his life.

His contempt of the world & fortitude in tribulations.

9. From this so excellent humility proceeded the contempt of himselfe, and of the world, and all wordly things which this Blessed Father had. For he who is truly humble, desireth to be humbled, and

taketh

taketh humiliation, as S: Bernard saith, for a meanes to obtayne humility. From the same humility likewise came his fortitude in troubles, and his patience in aduersities, and tribulations. For he, who is truly humble, dwelling within himselfe, accounteth himselfe so great a sinner, and so vnworthy of comfort, that he thinketh all to be too much for him, and that no euill happeneth vnto him, which seemeth not litle in comparison of that which he deserueth, and reioyceth to see all creatures take reuenge of him, as instruments of the diuine Iustice.

L 2 *Of*

Of his Mortifications , and Charity towards God.

CHAP. XIII.

NOvv what shall I say of the mortification of his passions, and of all inordinate affections, by which he had obtayned an admirable peace in his soul, and so great quietnes, and tranquillity, that nothing seemed able to disturbe him ? His complexion was very cholerike, but notwithstanding both in his words, and workes he was so mild, and sweet, that he seemed rather flegmatike, and of a cold complexion. So that hauing wholy ouercome the vicious

The mortification of his passions.

excesse

excesse of his choler , he retai-
ned the efficacy , and force
which it is wont to giue , and
is necessary for the execution
of such busines , as we deale
in . He alwayes kept one , and
the same tenour , and equality
in all things : and although
that of his body varied , yet
his mind , and inward disposition was alwayes one : neyther was he altered or changed with any diuersity of
things, or difference of tymes.
Yea this equality of mynd ,
and perpetuall constancy redounded in some sort to his
body , which was ready to receaue that outward demon-
stration which reason prescri-
bed .

2 . Being once sicke , the

Phisitian aduised him, that he should not giue place to such thoughts, as might afflict him. And with this occasion he began to examine, what thing in this world could cause him affliction; and after the consideration of many things he foūd this only one: If by some casuality our Society should be dissolued; and withall it seemed to him that if this fell out without his fault, after a little recollection in prayer for the space of one quarter of an houre, he should returne to his accustomed peace, and allacrity. Yea he added further, that he should haue his peace and quietnes in his soule, althought the Society were dissolued, as salt in the water.

How

How wholy then had he forsaken himselfe, and rooted himselfe in God, who in so great a matter, and so proper, and peculiar to himselfe was so subiect, and resigned to the will of our Lord? Which is an euident signe, that his passions were perfectly mortifyed.

3. By this mortification, and by that perfect knowledg, and contempt which he had of himselfe, this Blessed man, attayned to a most high, and excellent degree of charity, which is the summe of all vertues, and the complement of all perfection. This his burning, and enflamed loue towards God, appeared in nothing better, then in that, which he did, and suffered for

His charity toward God.

him . For true loue is neuer
idle, and is not content with
only doing much for his beloued , but in suffering much also, and giuing his life for him.
How much then did this Blessed Father , and what great
things did he suffer for our
Lords honour, and to amplify
his glory in the world ? Part
of it may be coniectured by
that, which hitherto hath byn
said .

4. But the Father himselfe
auouched , that all the things
of the world put togeather in
one ballance, were to him of
no esteeme , if in the other
were placed the fauours which
he had receyued of our Lord ,
in the persecutions , prisons,
and fetters which he had endured

dured for his loue. And that
there is no created thing,
which can cause so great a ioy
in a soule, as that is, which
she receiueth in hauing suffred
for Chrift. To which purpofe
being demaunded by a Father,
which was the shorteft, and
moft certayne, and secure way
to attayne perfection : he anfwered, that to endure many,
and very great aduerfityes for
the loue of Chrift. *Aske* (faid
he) *this grace of our Lord, for
to whom he doth it, he doth many
more togeather, which are contayned in it.* Thus the Bleffed
Father both did himfelfe
and taught others, by which
we may gather his great charity towards God.

5. But we haue other more

L 5   cleare

cleare arguments of this his
loue to God; and to his neighbours for the loue of God.
The scope to which all his a-
ctions, cares, and intentions
were directed, was *Gods grea-*
ter glory. For he contented not
himselfe, that God were not
offended in that he did, but
procured that he might be
glorified. And when two
things of Gods seruice offered
themselues vnto him, he did
alwayes choose that, out of
which he thought *Gods greater*
glory would ensue. And this
was, as we haue said, alwaies
his Poesy: and to this scope
he alwaies aymed. Many times
speaking with God from the
inmost of his hart, he said
vnto him : *O Lord, what do I*

desyre

desire, or can I desire besides thee?
And his desire to see him, and
to be dissolued from the prison of his body, was so great
and ardent, that when he
thought on his death he could
not refrayne from teares,
which distilled from his eyes
for pure ioy. And this not
only to obtayne that soueraigne good for himselfe, but
much more to behold the
glory of that most sacred humanity of the same Lord,
whom he loued so greatly; as
a friend is wont to reioyce
to see the honour, and glory
of him, whome he hartily
loueth.

6. In the yeare 1541 in
the moneth of Iuly (I being
present) he sayd, that if our

Lord

Lord God would giue him
his choife, eyther prefently to
depart out of this life, and to
enioy eternall happynes, or
to remaine in the world,
without hauing fecurity to
perfeuere in vertue; he would
choofe this fecond, if he might
vnderftand, that by remayning for fome fpace in this
life, he could doe fome great,
and notable feruice for his
Maiefty, cafting his eyes v-
pon God, and not vpon himfelfe, nor refpecting his owne
danger, or fecurity. And he
added the caufe: forwhat King
(faid he) or Prince is there in
the world, who if offering
fome great reward to one of
his feruants, he fhould refufe
to enioy it prefently, that

he

he might doe some notable
seruice for his Prince, would
not thinke himselfe obliged
to conserue, yea increase the
reward of that seruant, since
he depriued himselfe of it for
his loue, and that he might be
able to doe him more seruice?
And if mē proceed in this máner, what are we to hope for
of our Lord? or how can we
feare, that he will forsake vs,
or permit vs to fall, for hauing prolonged our happy-
nes,& differred to enioy him
for his sake? Let others thinke
so if they please (said he) for
I will not conceiue so hardly
of so good a God, and so gra-
tious, and soueraigne a King.

7. There came one tyme
to his mind a thought, what

he

he should thinke, if God should put him in hell: and he explicated his conceit in a paper written with his owne hand in this manner: *There were two things represented vnto me: the one, what paines I should suffer there: the other, how his Name was blasphemed. In the first I could not feele, nor find any affliction: and so me thought, and it was represented vnto me, that my greatest molestatiõ should be to heare his holy Name blasphemed.* These are his very words. Now what an enflamed loue did he beare to our Lord, who found this effect, and disposition in himselfe towards him? What flames of heauenly fire burned in that breast, since that those of the

fire

fire of hell could not quench them, nor make him feele affliction in his owne paynes, but only in the iniury, and offence of his beloued?

Of his Loue, and Charity towards his Neighbour.

CHAP. XIV.

FROM this ardent, and feruent loue towards God proceeded as from a foūtaine, the inflamed loue which he bare to his neighbours. For he beheld them in God, and God in them: and so he said that if it were profitable for the saluation of soules to go through the streets barefooted, and loaden with infamous

His charity toward his neyghbours.

mous

mous, & ignominious things, he would make no doubt to do it. And that there was no habit in the world so base and vile, which he would not willingly weare to gaine a soule.

2. In Paris he defired to deliuer a wicked man, who kept a Concubine, from that euill eftate: and diuers remedies which he had put in practice, taking no effect, he went one day into a Lake of exceeding colde water, by which the other was to paffe, and from thece he fpake aloud vnto him in thefe words: *Goe wretched creature to inioy thy filthy delights: feeft thou not the ftroke of Gods wrath which commeth vpon thee? Goe, for I will remayne here tormeting my felfe,*

and

and doing pennance for thee, vntill God releaſe his iuſt puniſhment: which is already prepared againſt thee. The man was amazed with ſo wonderfull an example of charity, he ſtayed, and being touched with Gods hand, returned back, forſaking that diſhoneſt company, to which he had beene captiue ſo long.

3. He obſerued alway with exceeding great care not to render any man euill, but ſtriued to do good to his perſecutors, procuring that his benefits towards them ſhould be greater, then the euills, & iniuries which he receiued from them. One of his fellow ſchollers who remained in the ſame houſe with him

His charity towards thoſe who did iniury or perſecute him.

M

him in Paris, ran away with
certaine money, which was
fent in almes to the B. Father,
and was committed to his cu-
ftody. Afterward this man
being in Roan, fell dange-
roufly fick, and knowing the
Fathers charity; wrote vnto
him, in what afflictió he was,
requefting him to take fome
order for his reliefe. The Father hauing made much and
earneft prayer for him, went
prefently to Roan (which is
28. leagues from Paris)to find
him out, & help him in what
he could, and with great alacrity of fpirit, and force of
mind, he went in three dayes
thofe 8. leagues barefoot,
without eating one bit of
bread, or drinking one drop

                              of

of water , offering this labour
and penance to our Lord , for
the health and life of him,
who had deceiued him in that
manner .

4. Another likewife, who
in Paris had receiued much
charity at the holy Fathers
hands, affaulted by Sathan, &
becomming as it were furious, refolued to kill him, and
being gone vp the ftayres for
that purpofe heard a dreadfull
voyce, which faid vnto him :
Thou wretch what wilt thou do?
who terrified with this voice,
caft himfelf at the Fathers feet
weeping , and related vnto
him, what his purpofe was .
The Father cherifhed , and
comforted him; but his charity , and meeknes was not

sufficient to with-hould this
very man from blowing the
coales of diuers calumniations & lyes afterward in that
storme, which (as we haue
said) was raised in Rome, before the Confirmation of the
Society: where the Iudges hauing punished him for that
cause, and the tempest being
past (to requite good for
euill) the Father receiued him
into the Society at the request
of those , who had raised that
persecution : but he perseuered not in his vocation. If
the B. Father dealt thus with
strangers, and with those that
pretended to do him iniury ,
what maruaile is there, that
he vsed the same charity with
his subiects, and children ?

5. One

5. One of the nine Fathers which came vnto him in Paris, being much afflicted & difquieted with a troublefome, and dangerous temptation, fo that he was in a manner loft; the B. Father deliuered him from that danger, by weeping bitterly, & praying to God continually for him, without eating, or drinking in three whole dayes, befeeching our Lord to comfort, and ftrengthen him: and fo he did. Another tyme another Father was much out of order, exceeding the bounds of reafon, by which meanes the holy Father was much grieued, and afflicted for the harme, which the other receiued. The reuenge which he

M 3 procu-

procured , was to put himfelfe
in prayer , and to fhed many
teares for him , and faying
Maffe , from the bottome of
his hart , he cryed, and fighed
vnto our Lord, faying: *Pardon*
him , O Lord , Pardon him , my
Creator, for he knoweth not what
he doth .

6 . Another tyme a Bro-
ther of the Society, being grie-
uoufly tempted in his vocation , and refolued to forfake
God , who is the fountayne of
liuing waters , and returne to
drinke of the broken cifternes
of the world , which containe
no water of grace , nor of true
repofe ; the Father vnderftanding that the caufe of that perturbation was the fhame, that
the brother had to confeffe a

finne

finne which he had committed , he went vnto him , and declared his former life , and how blynd he had byn in following the vanity of his fenfes and how much addicted to the falfe loue of creatures , that by this meanes the Brother might be leffe afhamed , and learne to haue a true cōceit of the goodnes , and mercy of our Lord .

7. Now what fhall I fay of the meekeneffe , and benignity , which he vfed towards all men , & efpecially to thofe, that were vnder his charge ? Of the care he had , leaft they fhould be ouerlayd ? Of the fweetenes wherewith he condefcended to the weake : rayfed thofe that were fallen: comforted the afflicted : en-

His meekeneffe, & berignity towards thofe who were vnder his charge.

M 4   coura-

couraged the faint-harted: and
tooke compaſſion of the diſea-
ſed , and ſickly ? For certainly
it was a thing which cauſed
admiration, to ſee the care that
he vſed , for the cure, and comfort of the ſicke . And he told
me ſometymes , that our Lord
had with particuler prouidence prouided that he ſhould
haue ſo little and vnperfect
health , that by his owne ſicknes & infirmityes , he might
learne to eſteeme thoſe of o-
thers , and take compaſſion of
the weake .

8. Being in Vincenza ſick
of an ague , he vnderſtood ,
that Father Symon Roderi-
quez, one of the Fathers, was
in Baſſana (about a dayes
iourney from Vincenza) very

sick,

sick, and in danger of death :
and presently the B. Father
tooke his iourney towards
Bassana , in the company of
Father Faber , to visit , and
comfort Father Symon , and he
went with such courage , and
force of spirit , that Father Faber could not follow him. Another tyme , being on the way ,
Father Laynes , who was with
him fell sudainly into a very
great payne , for remedy wherof , the Father presently sought
him , an horse , giuing six pence
for him , which was all the
money they had gotten of almes , and wrapping him in his
poore thrid-bare cloke he set
him vp , and ran before him
with such alacrity , & lightnes ,
that Father Laynes told me ,

M 5   he

he could scarce keep him company being on horsbacke.

9. But he discouered this his Fatherly loue towards. his children in nothing more then in prouiding for their good name, and spirituall profit, and in burying in perpetuall obliuion such faults as they committed, eyther by humane frailty, or negligence, when they themselues did acknowledg them with sorrow, and desire of amendement With this, and other louing, and Fatherly proceedings he did win the harts of all his children, and might do with them what he would, they were so subiect, tractable, and obedient to his will; and he prouoked them to his imitation in all

perfe-

perfection , and in that pure ,
fincere , and diuine loue of
our Lord in which it confi-
fteth .

10. Notwithftanding this
loue towards his children was
not feeble and remiffe , but
fweet and ftrong , mild and
feuere . For as he was fweete ,
and gentle with the humble
and obedient : fo he was terrible to the rebellious, and ftiff-
necked , hauing great care to
further his fubiects in vertue ,
and encourage them to perfection , vfing euery one mildly ,
or feuerely according to their
capacity, but yet fhewing loue
to all . And he was fo dextrous
in ioyning fweetnes with feuerity , that thought he defired
much to haue all his children

indiffe-

The Fa-
thers
loue was
fweet &
ftrong.

indifferent in matters of obedience, without inclination to any one thing more then to another , notwithstanding he examined the naturall dispofition of euery one with great diligence , and applyed himfelfe vnto them in all things , wherein he faw them to be well giuen . For he vnderftood, how troublefome that is, which is done with naturall repugnance , and that no violent thing is durable : fhewing his religious feuerity in requiring indifferency , and his Fatherly mildnes, and benignity in condefcending to their inclinations .

Of

*Of the particuler Deuotion, and
other vertues of B. F.
Ignatius.*

CHAP. XV.

VV E ſhould neuer make
an end, if we would
particulerly treate of the admirable charity of this glorious
Father, and of all his other vertues, which were without
number. Of his prudence rather diuine then humane,
which our Lord imparted vnto him, to the end he might
draw the whole frame of the
Society. Of his ſo excellent
fortitude and magnanimity to
vndertake great things, and
reſiſt contradictions, and difficulties.

His o-
ther ver-
tues.

ficultyes . Of his mildnes, and
meekenes with which he did
ioyne the harts of thofe that
treated with him ., changing,
and bending the wills, and affections of his very aduerfa-
ryes. What fhall I fay of his
Vigilancy, and admirable follicitude in bringing to an end
the workes, which he did vndertake? For he did not only
feeke out with prudence what
meanes might help him to the
compaffing of them, but hauing found them he vfed them
with great efficacy, neuer giuing ouer that which he had
once begun , vntill he had
brought it to perfection.

2 . What fhould I fay of
the wonderfull confidence ,
which he had alwayes in God?

In his imprisonments that he
would protect him : in his labours that he would help him :
in his difficult enterprises, that
he would perfect them with
his powerfull hand? And in
his pouerty, that he would relieue him, and sustayne his
children, as he did many tymes
miraculously, shewing that the
hope of this holy Father had
not byn in vayne? What shall I
say of the modesty, and efficca-
cy of his words? What of his
auoyding to iudge, or con-
demne other mens liues? What
of his circumspection in speaking or hearing others speak
of their neighbours faults,
thought they were publicke,
and talked of in the very streetes? What of his warines and

wisdome,

wifdome, with which he inter-
rupted all fpeaches, that might
be occafion, though neuer fo
light or fmall, of any murmu-
ration? What of the other vertues which he had , and all fo
perfect , as if he had only one,
and with fuch eminency , that
no man knoweth in which of
them he excelled moft ? But
let vs omit them al, to fpeak of
that vertue which is the guide,
and miftreffe of the reft, & the
paffage or conduct , by which
our Lord imparteth his giftes
to our foules, that is Prayer, &
Deuotion , and the familiar
connerfation with his Diuine
Maiefty .

3. The Father himfelf có-
feffed, that our Lord had large-
ly imparted vnto him the grace

of

of deuotion, which he for
his humility attributed to his
own weaknes, & misery; because being now old, sickly, &
wearyed, he was good for nothing, but to giue himselfe
wholy to God. Presently after
he was made Priest, when he
said the Diuine Office, the a-
boundannce of Gods comfort
was so great, and the teares,
which he shed so many, that
he was enforced to stay almost
in euery word, and to interrupt the houres, or part of the
office, which he said: And this
went so far, that he had almost
lost his sight with weeping In
matters of importance, he was
neuer wont to take any resolution, though he had neuer
so many probable reasons, be.

N   fore

fore he had commended them
to our Lord in Prayer . There
was no houre in the day, in
which he did not inwardly recollect himselfe , and setting
aside all other businesses, examined his conscience : and if
peraduenture some great, or
vrgent businesse permitted
him not to fullfil his deuotion
in one houre, he did presently
recompence it so soone as he
might : albeit he neuer gaue
himselfe so much to outward
affayres , that he lost the inward deuotion of his spirit .

4 . He had God alway
present before his eyes in all
things, and they all serued
him for a booke to read his
diuine perfections in , and to
eleuate his hart to him, draw-

ing

ing spirituall documents, and
profitable aduises out of euery
thing that he did see; teaching
that this manner of prayer is
very profitable for all, principally for those who are imployed in exteriour things belonging to Gods seruice. Before his prayer he prepared his
soule, and entred into the O-
ratory of his hart, and there
he inflamed himselfe in such
sort, that it appeared in his
countenance, and he seemed
to be all set on fire, as we no-
ted, & discouered many tymes.
He vsed such attention in euery thing, though neuer so litle,
belonging to his conuersation
with God, and he was so recollected, and present in himselfe when he did it, that he

seemed

seemed to behold the Maiesty
of God present, as when he
said grace before, or after meat
and in other like occasions.

5. He had a very excellent
gift of teares, which he shed
in great aboundance in his
prayers, with great ioy of his
spirit, and no lesse harme to
his body; of which he made
no account, that he might not
loose the spirituall fruit of his
soule. But finally ouercome
with reason, and because the
Phistians shewed him, how
much that continuall effusion
of teares did hurt his health, he
beseeched our Lord to giue
him the maistery, and commaund ouer them. And he obtayned it so entirely, that he
seemed to haue them in his

hand

hand to fhed, or repreffe them
when, and how it pleafed him
And this with fo great fauour
of the diuine Mercy , that
though his eyes were dry , yet
his fpirit remayned alwayes
moift , and his heauenly illuftrations were not diminifhed,
how much-foeuer his teares
were moderated by reafon, but
their fruit remained in all force
and vigour. No noife , how
great foeuer it were, did trouble or hinder him in his prayer
if he had giuen no occafion
therof. But any obftacle what-
foeuer was an impediment vnto him , if it were in his power
to auoid it , fo that, it was not
the noife, but the negligence,
which he feemed to haue committed , in not taking away,

that which difquietted him at his prayer. The B, Father him-felfe being once, demaūded by Father Laynes of the manner of his prayer, gaue him this an-fwere : that in matters concer-ning our Lord, he found him-felfe rather *Paſſiuely* then *Actiuely* (for thefe are the words which the contemplatiue, and thofe who treat of this matter do vfe:) accounting this the higheft degree of contempla-tion; in the fame fort, that S. Dionyfius Areopagita, fpea-king of his mafter Hierotheus, fayth of him : *Erat patiens Di-uina*.

His de-
uotiō to
our B.
Lady.

6. He was exceedingly deuout to the moft Sacred Vir-gine Mary our B. Lady, whom from the tyme that he opened

his

his eyes to behold the light of
heauen, he alwayes tooke for
his especiall Patronesse & Aduocate; hauing recourse to her
in all his necessityes, difficultyes, and labours; and receyuing great graces, and fauours
from her mighty, and bountifull hand ; as may be gathered
by that, which we haue said
hitherto, and shall appeare by
that which we will say heare-
after.

Of his diuine Reuelations , and
Contemplations in God .

CHAP. XVI.

BVT what meruaile was it,
that he should giue himself
so much to prayer, who was

What
reuela-
tionshe
had.

so greatly fauoured by God in
his prayers, and that he should
be absorpt in contemplation,
who was illustrated with so
many diuine visitations, and
reuelations? For from the tyme
of his first sicknes, and before
he was conuerted from the vanity of the world to our Lord,
his diuine Maiesty began to
fauour him, and sent him (as
we haue said) his Apostle S.
Peter, in his greatest daunger,
to restore him his health. And
after that he had put himselfe
vnder the banner of our Lord
Iesus Christ, fearing the
weakenes of his flesh, the most
Excellent, and Soueraigne
Queene of Angels, hauing her
most pretious Sonne in her
armes appeared vnto him, as

he

he was awake, and with the
splendor of her glory enlight-
ned him, with the sweetnes
of her presence recreated and
strengthned him, blotting out
of his soule (as it were with
her hand) all vncleane cogita-
tions, and dishonest represen-
tations.

2. In the tyme, that he
remayned at Manresa, afflic-
ting himselfe with such austere penances (as hath beene
related) after he had passed
those torments, tentations,
and scruples, which brought
him so low, and to such extre-
mity; our Lord comforted
and cherished him, with his
soueraigne, and heauenly visitations. For sitting one day
vpon the steps of S. Domi-

N 5   nicks

nicks Church, saying the Office of our B. Lady with much deuotion, our Lord illustrated his vnderstanding, and represented vnto him, as it were a figure of the most holy Trinity, which exteriourly signified vnto him, that, which interiourly he perceiued: & this with such aboundāce of comfort, that he could not represse his sobs, and teares, nor thinke or speake of any thing, but of the mystery of the most Holy Trinity, with so many similitudes, and examples, that all who heard him, remayned much admired, and astonished. And from that tyme forward, this inefable mystery was so imprinted in his soule, that euen then

he

he began to write a booke of
this profound matter, which
contayned 80. leaues, knowing at that tyme no more then
only to write, and read . And
after likewise the intelligence
which he had of the most B.
Trinity, the Diuine Essence,
the distinction and propriety
of the three Persons was so
continuall, excellent, and ab-
stract, that the B. Father himselfe in a Note-booke of his
owne hand (which was
found after his death) sayth ,
that he could not haue
knowne so much with many
years study. And in another
place he sayth, that it seemed
to him , that there was no
more to be knowne in this
life of those matters of the

most

most Holy Trinity, then our Lord had imparted vnto him in a certaine vision.

3. But returning to Manresa another tyme with great ioy of his spirit, he had represented vnto him the manner which God obserued in creating the world. Another tyme hearing Masse in the Monastery of S. Dominicke, at the tyme of eleuation, he did clearly see with the eyes of his soule, that vnder that veile, and forme of bread, our Lord Iesus Christ true God and Man was truly couered, and contayned. Many tymes being in prayer, and for a good space, with the same inward eyes of his soule, he did behould the sacred Humanity

of

He seeth Christ in the B. Sacrament, & in his Humanity, with our B. Lady.

of our Sauiour Iesus Christ.
And some tymes likewise the
most glorious Virgin Mary
his mother: and this not only
in Manresa, but also after he
was departed from thence
neere to Padua, and at Hierusalem, and in many other
places.

4. He went once out of
Manresa to pray in a certaine
Church, distant from that
towne a little mile, and in the
way being transported, and
eleuated in contemplation
of our Lord, he sate him
downe vpon the banke of the
riuer, not far from the way,
and casting the eyes of his
body vpon the water, those
of his soule were opened, and
illuminated with a new, and

*He is il-
lustra-
ted and
taught
by God.*

vowon-

vnwonted light, not so, that
he did see any sensible shape,
or figure, but after another
more high, and intelligible
manner. With this light, he
vnderstood very perfectly
many things, aswell of those
which appertayned to the
mysteries of our faith, as of
other, which belong to the
knowledge of sciences: in so
much, that the same things,
that he had seene before seemed afterward not to be the
same. And this Diuine rapt,
and suspention endured for a
good space.

His exta-
sis of
eight
dayes.

5.   But that other accident
which happened vnto him
while he was yet in Manresa
is more to be admired. For v-
pon a Saturday, at the tyme

of

of Complyne , he remayned
so alienated , and bereaued of
his senses, that he was held
for dead: and they had buryed
him, if they had not discerned
that his hart did still beate
though very weakly. He continued in this rapt or Extasy
vntill Saturday of the weeke
following, at the same tyme
of Compline, when many be
ing present who obserued
him, he opened his eyes, as if
he had awaked out of a sweet,
and pleasant sleepe, and with
a still, and louing voyce, said.
O I E S V . And this is testified by those who were witnesses of it , or at least heard
it related by them who were
present .

6 . That reuelation which he

had

had at his comming to Rome
(as we said before) was very
notable, when being at his
prayers in a Church, the Eternal Father appeared vnto him,
and his Bleſſed Sonne with his
Croſſe vpō his ſhoulders, who
ſpake vnto him theſe moſt cō-
fortable words; *Ego vobis Ro-*
mæ propitius ero. Likewiſe being
at Monte Caſſino (where S.
Benedict did ſee the ſoule of S.
German Biſhop of Capua, caryed by Angells in a globe of
fyre to Heauen, as S. Gregory
writeth) the B. Father beheld
the ſoule of Bachelour Hozius,
who came vnto him at Ve-
nice, go vp to heauen, and he
knew that it was the ſoule of
Hozius one of his Society, who
being in the Citty of Padua

with

How
Chriſt
appea-
red vnto
him.

with Father Iohn Codury. paſſed to a better life . And when
the ſame Father Iohn Codury
died in Rome, vpon the day of
the Decollation of S . Iohn
Baptiſt , in the yeare of our
Lord 1541. the B . Father going that morning before he
dyed, to ſay Maſſe for him at
the Monaſtery of S . Peter *de
Monte aureo*, which is on the
other ſide of the riuer of Ty-
bur, while he was paſſing the
bridge called of Sixtus, he ſaw
the ſoule of Father Iohn Codury, which went to heauen
with great glory : and turning
himſelfe to Father Iohn Baptiſt a Viola, who accompanied
him, and told me of it, he ſaid:
*Father Iohn Codury is now de-
parted*

O   7. Father

7.   Father Leonard Keſſel borne in Flaunders, was one of the ancient Fathers of that Prouince, and a very great ſeruant of God, and ſo accounted in the Society. I knew him in Cullen, where he laid the firſt foundations of the Colledge which we haue there, & did gouerne it many yeares with great fame, and opinion of ſanctity. This Father Leonard deſyred much to ſee, and conuerſe with his B. Father, & Maiſter, Ignatius. He wrote vnto him, asking leaue to go on foot from Cullen to Rome, which is aboue 300. leagues, only to ſee him, and enioy his holy communication. The Father anſwered him, that his preſéce was neceſſary in Cul-

len

len for Gods seruice , & there-
fore willed him not to remoue
from thence; for our Lord
could so ordayne , that he
might see him without vndertaking so long, and difficult a
iourney . After which Father
Leonard being in Cullen, the
Holy Father Ignatius appeared vnto him on a tyme being
awake while he was yet aliue,
& stayed for some space there
present with him : and when
he departed , he left Father
Leonard very much cóforted
for hauing obtayned his desire
in so strange, and maruelous a
manner .

. 8. To Iohn Paschall sonne
of Agnes Paschall (who was
wont euery morning to go to
the first Masse , which is said

in the Chappell of S. Eulalia,
in the Cathedrall Church of
Barcelona, vnder the high
Altar) he appeared one morning before the fame high Altar, fome yeares after his death:
and Iohn Pafchall knew him,
and faid vnto him, *O my Father*, going towards him; but
the B.Father made him a figne
with his hand, that he fhould
come no neerer, and fo departed. He had other vifitations,
and fauours of our Lord like
vnto thefe, and wrought o-
ther meruails, which we omit
to auoid prolixity. But that,
which caufed vs, who knew
and conuerfed with this Holy
Father, moft admiration, is:
that thefe fauours of our Lord
being fo ordinary, and dayly

(as may be feene in the pa-
pers, which he wrote with his
owne hand, when he made
the Conftitutions, and were
found after his death) we
fcarfe euer heard him fpeake,
or make any mention of any
reuelation, vifion, rapt, exta-
fie, or other thing of this kynd:
but only of humility, charity, patience, contempt of himfelfe, zeale of Gods glory, labouring for the good of foules,
prayer, mortification, & other
fuch vertues of which he made
great account. For thefe be
fuch as make men, Saints,
and friends of God : and thofe
other things, though they
fhyne more in the eyes of men,
are but fignes, and not alwaies
certayne, of fanctity & grace.

Of certaine beames of Glory seene about B. F. Ignatius Head; & how he was indued with the gift of Prophecy.

CHAP. XVII.

The Fathers head, & countenãce become resplendent.

NOT only the soule of this Seruant of our Lord was illustrated with the visitatiõs, and fauours which we haue mentioned: but part of thatfulnes, which the soule receiued, redounded likewise to his body. Whereupon many tymes, diuers looking vpon him, did see his countenance resplendent, and casting forth bright beames; as it happened in Barcelona to Elizabeth Rosell,

when

whē the B. Father sate among
the children on the steps of
the Altar, as we haue said: and
to Iohn Paschall, the sonne
of Agnes Paschall, who kept
him in his house a long tyme,
in the same Citty of Barcelona: and in Loyola, when he
went from Paris, and lyued in
the Hospitall, others did see
the same. And at Rome the B.
Father Philip Nereus, a man of
knowne sanctity; & the founder of the Oratory of those venerable Priests of our Blessed
Lady *De Nauicula*, which hath
done so much good in that
Citty (with whome I was very wel acquainted) was a most
deuout child of our B. Father
Ignatius, and came to him for
counsell in all his doubts, and

O 4 per

perplexityes : and when he
was sad , did feele his heart
lightned , and reioyced with
only seeing him , & was wont
to recount that he had many
tymes seene him with a light
about his head, which did cast
bright beames from it . This
B. Father deceased the 26. day
of May in the yeare 1595. and
vpon his day and memory, his
Children make a great feast .

2. But that is more notable,
which happened to Alexander
Petronius, a famous & much
esteemed Phisitian of Rome ,
and a great friend of our B.
Father, who being once grieuously sicke, Father Ignatius
went to visit him , and entred
into the sick mans chamber ,
which was very darke, all the

win-

windowes being shut; and at his entrance it was replenished with a new light, which Alexander did see, and demaunded of his wife, what light that was; and presently he felt himselfe well, attributing this benefit to the Blessed Fathers presence. And though he dissembled the matter at that tyme, passing it ouer in silence; yet after the B. Fathers departure to a better life, he did publishe, and manifest it with great admiration, and esteeme of his Holynesse. In o-other places likewise he was seene with this supernaturall light and splendor, and in Barcelona Iohn Paschall often beheld him in prayer eleuated in the ayre, a foote & more aboue

the

the ground, speaking with God, and saying: *O my God, O my Lord, O that men knew thee.*

3.   Our Lord likewise imparted vnto him the gift of Prophecy, so that being illustrated with a Diuine light, he foretold many things long before they fell out. At the tyme that he departed from Manresa towards Ierusalem, Iohn Paschall aforesaid who then was but a youth about eightene Yeares old, would haue accompanied him; but the Father willed him to returne, & assist his Mother; further telling him, that he should marry, & haue children, togeather with many troubles, and molestations counselling him to

be are

He had the gift of Prophecy.

beare them with patience and
the like: all which came to
paſſe, as the Father had foretold.

4. Being in Flanders, whither he went ſometymes from
Paris to aske almes for his ſu-
ſtenance (as hath been ſaid
before)dyning one day at Ant-
werp with certaine merchants
who had inuited him, he caſt
his eyes vpon one of them,
who was ſomewhat far off, a
young man,called Peter Quadratus, borne in *Medina del
Campo.* And beholding him attentiuely, he bad him come
neerer for being to be ſo great
a benefactor of the Religion of
the Society of Ieſus, it was fitting, that they ſhould preſently come acquainted, and take

notice

notice one of another : adding
that he had great reason to
thanke God, because he would
vouchfafe to vfe him, making
him the founder of a Colledge
of the Society (this being fo
long before the Society it felf,
began) all which was veri-
fyed. For many yeares after
Peter Quadratus , and Doña
Francifca Manjona his wife
founded the Colledg , which
the Society hath at this prefent
in *Medina del Campo*.

5. When the Father went
from Vincenza to Baffana , to
vifit Father Symon , who was
very fick , and in danger , hauing in his company Father
Faber , leauing him vpon the
way , he went a litle afide to
pray for Father Symon, and in

his

his prayer was certifyed, that
he should not die of that sicknes , as he told Father Faber
at his returne. And comming
to the place where the sicke
man was , he imbraced him
saying: *Feare not , Brother Sy-*
mon , you shall not dye at this
tyme; & with these words he
presently recouered , as the
same F.Symon often testifyed,
and Father Faber related it to
Father Laynes, who remay-
ned sicke at Vincenza , of
whom I knew it.

6. Likewise in Bassana one
of the Fathers began to doubt
of his vocation , and whether
it were not better to remayne
in the copany of an Hermite,
who liued a very Holy life, giuing himselfe to contempla-

tion

tion, then to follow the B.
Father, and imploy himselfe
in helping the soules of his
neighbours. And going one
day to consult this doubt with
the Hermite himselfe, he had
great visions, and was much
terrifyed in the way: and comming in that feare, and out of
breath, into the lodging,
where Father Ignatius was, he
with the light of Heauen knowing what he had in his
breast, said vnto him; *Modicæ
fidei quare dubitasti?* Man of
of litle faith why didst thou
doubt? And he was confirmed
with these words, & perseuered vntill death in his vocation.

7. In the yeare 1541. Stephen Baroelus an Italian, en

tred

tred into the Society at Rome, and not long after fell dangerously ficke, whereupon the Phificians hauing in a manner giuen him ouer, our Bleſſed Father went to S. Peter *de Monte aureo* to ſay Maſſe for him. I did accompany him that day (as I vſed to do many other tymes)and I ſerued him at Maſſe: which being ended, and after he had giuē thankes, he ſaid to me: *Stephen ſhall not dye at this tyme.* And he preſently recouered, and went afterward to Portugall, and returned back againe to Italy, and liued many yeares, and finally made an holy end in the Society.

8. Doctour Arrouira a very Honorable Cittizen of

Barce-

Barcelona , who a few yeares
since came to Madrid for Embassadour of that Citty ; to
King Philip the second , who
is now in glory, tould me that
being in Rome, he had much
acquaintance , and familiarity
with the Blessed Father , and
that one day comming from
Ara Cæli, he met him in the
street with a letter in his hand,
which was giuen him from
Don Fracisco de Borgia, Duke
of Gandia , who at that tyme
was marryed , and Viceroy of
Cataluña , and that speaking
of that letter, which he had receyued , he said: *Little would
you thinke, that this Noble man,
who hath written this letter, shall
come to Rome , to be the head of
our Religion* . Which was fulfilled

led afterward, when the Dutchesse his wife being dead, the Duke entred into the Society, and hauing byn many yeares Cōmissary Generall in Spaine, in the yeare 1565. vpon the day of the Visitation of our Blessed Lady, the second of Iuly, he was chosen to be the third Generall.

9. And the same Doctor Michaell Arrouira affirmed, that he being then a young man, and in doubt what state of life to choose, afterward he determined to marry: and before he told the Father his resolution (for he kept it secret) the Father himselfe said vnto him. *I know well inough, that you are resolued to marry; O how you will bewayle it, and in what troubles*

P   *will*

will you see your selfe. All which fell out in that manner: and this which he reported to me, he also affirmed vpon his oath, as a witnes before the Bishop of Barcelona. When Agnes Paschal dyed, they sent him word of her death to Rome, that he might commend her to God: and he answered, that before the receipt of the letter, he knew, that she was departed, and in heauen.

10. Father Laynes being in Venice, procuring that that Common Wealth would put vs in possession of the Priory of S. Mary Magdalen in the Citty of Padua (which Pope Paul the third had vnited to the Colledge of the Society there) found very great difficulties,

and

and potent aduerſaryes: in ſo
much, that he in a manner deſ-
payred of that buſines: wher-
upon he wrote to the Bleſſed
Father, requeſting him to ſay
a Maſſe, that God would giue
him good ſucceſſe, which he
expected not by humane
meanes. The Father ſaid the
Maſſe vpon the Natiuity of
our Lady, and wrote to Father
Laynes in theſe words: *I haue
done that which you deſired: be of
good courage, and take no care for
this buſines; for you may well account it ended according to your
deſire.* As the Father wrote, ſo
it came to paſſe; for vpon the
octaue of the ſame Natiuity of
our B. Lady, the Counſell met
which in Venice is called *Pre-
gai,* and in a manner all the Se-

nators with one accord agreed
that we should haue the possession giuen vs, to the great admiration of those, who had
experience in the gouerment
of that Common Wealth. He
likewise told the same Father
Laynes, that he should succeed
him in the office of Generall,
and so he did.

11. In the yeare 1555.
sending the Fathers Hierome
of Nadall, and Lewys Gonsa-
lez de Camera to Spayne, he
willed them to ship themselues
presently at Genua, for without doubt, they should haue a
prosperous nauigation; and so
they had, though it were in
winter. The German Colledg
being in extreme necessity,
and without hope of remedy,

in

in so much that the Cardinalls
who had care of it, were so dif-
mayed , that they counselled
the blessed Father not to weary
himselfe in so disperat a matter:
he answered , that he would
not giue it ouer , and that the
tyme would come, in which
that Colledge should be suffici-
ently prouided , and stored of
all necessaryes. And so it was.
For the Holynesse of Pope
Gregory the XIII. endowed,
& founded it liberally, so that
now it hath completly all
things needfull .

12 . The like succeded in
the prouision of the Roman
Colledg of the Society, which
being in great want , and not
knowing by any humane
means, from whence, or how

to be prouided , the Father betooke himselfe to prayer , and
after told certayne Fathers ,
that there was no care to be taken for that busines : and that
within a few moneths , our
Lord would prouide for it , as
he did, & sometymes as it were
miraculously , vntill the same
Pope Gregory the XIII. of
holy memory , founded it . He
foretold other things like to
these , before they happened :
all which were fulfilled , as he
said , and I omit them for breuity .

Of

Of the Miracles of B. F. Igna-
tius: And first of his power
ouer Diuells, as well in
his life, as after
his death.

CHAP. XVIII.

BESIDES the gift of Pro-
phecy, which our Lord
imparted to this holy Father,
he also gaue him the grace to
do many, and great Miracles,
both whilst he liued, and after
his deceafe. Some of thofe I
meane to touch briefly in this
place, but not all (for that
would be too long) which our
Lord hath wrought by this his
feruant. For though when I
firft fet forth his life in Latyn,

which was in the yeare 1572.
I had notice of some other miracles of the holy Father, then
those that I there set downe:
yet I knew them not so certainly, that I thought it fit to
publish them: but since, with
the authenticall informations,
which haue byn taken for his
Canonization, they haue byn
proued by sufficient witnesses:
and our Lord, who will exalt
and make him glorious vpon
earth doth euery day so many
miracles by his meanes, that I
am obliged to declare some
part of them heere, taking
them out of the Authenticall
and Iuridicall Informations,
which many Prelates haue
made, and are at this tyme in
my hands; and out of the de

posi-

positions , which the partyes themselues , on whom these miracles haue byn wrought , haue made vnder their corporall oaths , & by the testimony of others, who deserue credit .

2. First then, he had great dominion , and commaund ouer the Diuels , and they abhorred , and persecuted him , as theyr cruell enemy ; fearing him in that respect and declaring him to be so . For in the tyme that he remayned in Manresa , the Diuell appeared vnto him many tymes in a shyning , and beautifull figure , till at length illustrated with diuine light , he knew , that it was the Diuell , who would deceiue him . And not only in Manresa , but also in his iour-

What hatred the Diuels bare him, & what dominion our Lord gaue him ouer them

P 5 neyes,

neyes, and at Parys, & Rome,
he appeared many tymes vnto
him, but so contemptible, and
deformed, that not making
any account of him, he did
easely driue him away with the
staffe which he had in his hand
(as if he had byn a cat, or a
little dogge.) This malignant
spirit procured to terrify him
whilst he remayned in the hospitall of Lewis de Antecaña
in Alcala, but he could not
preuaile. He would also haue
choked him another tyme at
Rome in his sleep, & he throt-
led him in such sort, that he
was inforced to inuocate, and
call vpon the sweet name of
Iesus, with so great a force,
that he remayned hoarse many
dayes after.

3. Another tyme being in his bed , the Diuells did ſtrike and beat him , and a brother called Iohn Paul of Cataluña who was his companion (and told me of it) heard him, and roſe twice to helpe , and aſſiſt him ; but they could do him no harme , becauſe our Lord permitted them not. They ac-counted him their mortal ene-my, who made cruell warre v-pon them , & tooke the ſoules out of their clawes ; and they publiſhed many tymes, that he was the greateſt enemy , which they had vpon earth.

4. In the yeare 1541. I my ſelfe heard a Diuell, which tormented a poore young man in Rome called Matthew, ſay, that he deſired vs not to ſpeak

of

of Ignatius, becaufe he was
the greateft enemy he had.
Another fouldier poffeffed in
the Citty of Padua ; and a woman in the Citty of Trapana
in Sicily faid as much. By reafon of this hatred, and enimi-
ty of the Diuells towards him,
they perfecuted him fo much ;
and raifed fo many, and fo
furious blafts, and tempefts a-
gainft him, which argued their
great anger, and malice; but
by the grace of our Lord, he
ouercame them all, & fubdued
them with fo great dominion,
as may be gathered by that
which we fhall here declare.

5. At the tyme that he remayned in the hofpitall of *Az-*
peritia (as hath byn faid before)
by reafon of the fame of his

sanctity, they brought a woman vnto him, who had byn possessed foure yeares, that he would exorcize her, and pray vnto God for her. He answered with much humility, that he was no Priest, nor deserued so much at our Lords hands; but that he would pray to his diuine Maiesty for her, which he did, and the woman was presently deliuered. At Rome, he cured that forsaid young man, called Matthew, who was greuously tormented by the Diuell, by only speaking vnto him, and shutting himselfe with him alone in a chamber. I knew him both before, and after, and he became religious in the wildernesse of Camaldula, and was

called

He casteth out a Diuell at Azperitia and also one at Rome

And another at Rome.

called Fryar Baſill.

6. In the yeare 1554. the Colledge of the Society which we haue at our B . Ladyes of Loreto was begun , and the firſt Rector therof was Father Oliuerius Manaræus, who liueth at this day in Flanders , a man of great religion , & very well knowne in that reſpect in the Society: who teſtifyeth , that the Diuells beganne preſently to make warre vpon our Fathers which dwelt in that Colledge, & to diſquiet them day, and night; ſometyme making a great ſtirre , and noiſe , others times appearing in diuers ſhapes, and formes, as of a blacke-More , or of a dog, or cat , or other beaſt , not permitting them to repoſe , and

ſleep

He freeth the Colledg of Loreto from the moleſtation of the Diuells.

sleep in the night; and that hauing vsed all possible meanes
of Masses, prayers, holy-water,
exorcismes, reliques, and o-
ther like, without profit, to
deliuer themselues from that
trouble, and importunity of
the Diuells; he wrote what had
passed to Blessed Father Ignatius, crauing the help and fauour of his prayers: who answered, that they should trust
in the goodnes of our Lord,
that he would deliuer them,
and he in their behalf would
intreat the same very instantly.

7. When Father Oliuerius
had receyued this letter, he
presently called togeather all
the Fathers, and brethren of
the Colledge, and read vnto
them, what the Father had

written,

written, and from that houre (a meruailous thing) all thofe troubles, and fearefull reprefentations of the Diuells ceafed, in fuch fort that there was no more figne of them, then if there had neuer byn any fuch thing. This happened while our Bleffed Father was aliue. But prefently after his death, there was a woman in the Citty of Trapana in Sicily exorcized, being tormented by the Diuell, and the Viceroy Iohn de Vega (who had newes of the Fathers defceafe, though it were not yet publifhed) caufed them to demaūd, where B. Father Ignatius the founder of the Society of Iefus was? And the Diuell anfwered: that his enemy Ignatius

The Diuell confeffeth that the Father is his enemy.

was

was now dead, and in heauen
with the other Founders of
Religions S. Dominicke, and
S. Francis.

3. In the yeare 1561. I
knew, in the Citty of Siena
in Italy, a very vertuous, and
simple mayd called Iacoba de
Prado, seruant to a Lady,
who was Aunt to the Arch-
bishop of the same Citty.
This mayd was very much
tormented, and persecuted by
the Diuells, who appeared
vnto her in diuers shapes, mis-
using, striking, and beating
her in very strang, and cruell
manner. The poore maid endured this torment for the
space of twelue yeares, vntill
she began to carry with her a
picture of our Blessed Father

The Fathers picture deliuereth a maid from the Diuells cruelty.

Q   Igna-

Ignatius : and presently the
Diuells, though they visibly
appeared vnto her, and cryed
out, saying: that he was their
enemy, willing her to cast a-
way that picture ; yet they
durst not come night her, nor
touch her : yea shewing them
the picture, they cast downe
their eyes, saying : that they
could not behold so bad a
thing : and though shee prouoked them to strike her, if
they could, yet they neuer
durst do it, so long as she kept
the picture.

9. At one tyme desirous
for curiosity to be certified,
whether that feare of the Diuells proceeded from the picture of the Blessed Father, or
from some other cause, she

layd

layd it aside , and presently
they came vpon her , beating
her so terribly , that they left
her dead . And this happened
vnto her another tyme long
after , she thinking , that she
had byn wholy free . And
with this experience she resol
ued not to bereaue herselfe
of that strong brest-plate and
buckler of the Blessed Fathers
picture , which terrifyed the
Diuells in that manner , who
not being able to strike her
gaue great blowes vpon the
chamber walls, and vpon certayne coffers, & cheits which
were in it . without euer tou
ching any one wherein there
was a picture of the Blessed
Father .

10   The same in a manner

happened in the Citty of Ancona in the yeare 1599. to a
Schole-maister called Leopar-
lus. For he perceyuing certaine spirits to frequent his
howse, who in the beginning,
while he was abfent, swept his
chaber, made his bed, brought
ight, and afterward diforde-
red, and fouled it againe ;
placed a picture of the Blessed
Father in his chamber, and
afterward found no moleftat-
iō in it. But without the dores
they made a great noise, ope-
ning & shutting them, & the
windowes, and striking as
vpon drummes ; but by pla-
cing the picture of the Blessed
Father in those roomes allo, all
that ftir ceased, & he was not
troubled any more.

11. In Rome the yeare 1597. the eight day of Iuly there being an exorcilme in a Church, Father Iohn Baptista Perulco of the Society of Iesus came in to say his prayers hauing a Reliquary, in which among many other reliques, there was one of the Blessed Father. He was no sooner come in, but the diuell began to cry out, and say, that the Father did burne him with that which he brought about him: and finally being inforced with the exorcilmes, he confessed, that the reliques which that Priest had at this breast, were of Blessed Father Ignatius, a great Seruant of God, and founder of the religion of the Society of Iesus: &

Q 3   that

that he was a Saynt in heauen,
though not yet knowne, but
ere long he should be canonized on earth: and the said Father Perusco taking the Reliquary from about his neck &
laying it vpon the possessed
woman, the Diuell gaue great
shoutes, saying, that the Relique of that Father burned
him, and so he left the woman free, it being our Lords
pleasure, that shee should re-
ceyue that notable fauour by
the intercession of the Blessed
Father.

Another
Diuell
cast out
in Ma-
jorca.

12.   In the Citty of Ma
jorca a womã called Catharin
Roca, was for the space of
eleuen yeares, almost euery
day grieuously tormented by
the Diuell. He made her beat

h:r

her hands, and head against
the wall; he lifted her vp in
the ayre, he made her body fo
heauy, that diuers ftrong men
could not lift her from the
ground. Sometymes fhe how-
led like a dog, and other tymes
grunted like a fwyne: and likewife fhe was fomtymes without iudgment or fenfe, foa
ming at her mouth. Yt was a
pittiful thing to fe her with-ut
remedy, hauing aplyed many,
vntill the yeare 1598. the laft
of Auguft, a Prieft called Iohn
Peé tooke a fubfcription of
Bleffed Father Ignatius, and
layd it vpon the poffeffed woman, who at that tyme was
depriued of her fenfes; & fhe
vfed great extremityes, making many motions and vi-

Q 4   fages

ages, and the Diuell presently
eparted, and left her, the re-
nayning free, and returning
o her former, and naturall
health, retyring her self to giue
our Lord thanks for the fauour
receyued at his Blessed hands
by the meanes of his seruant
Ignatius.

13. In *Monti-cala* which
is a towne in the territory of
Siena, there was a mayd called Vlna, and her fathers name
was Graiian Gala: who in
the moneth of Iuly the yeare
1599. was much afflicted by
he Diuells, who appeared vnto her in corporal shapes, speaking vnto her, and solliciting
her to filthy, and dishonest
things, to which when shee
would not consent, they did

beat

Also an-
other
dispos-
sessed in
the coū-
try of
Siena.

beat her cruelly, leauing the
signes and scars of their blowes vpon her brused body :
but our Lord deliuered her by
meanes of the picture of Blessed Father Ignatius .

Of foure Sisters of Modena dis-
possessed of Diuells by the
Meritts of B . F .
Ignatius.

CHAP. XIX.

BVt that is more notable
& declareth more the Do
minion which our Lord hath
giuen to this his Seruant , ouer
the Diuells, which happened
in the yeare 1600 in Modena,
a Citty of Lumbardy, which I
wil relate heere in the same mã-

Q 5   ner,

ner, that it hath beene written from thence, though briefly, and in fewer wordes yet with more then I am wont, because it is so notable a thing There were in that Citty of Modena foure sisters, noble, and honest women, one wherof was maryed & the other three mayds: al which together with a niece of theirs (likewise a maide) were for many yeares tormented with a great multitude of malignant spirits : & this with such rigour , that it was a very pittifull thing to see the manifold, & diuers vexatiōs which they cōtinually suffered of the Diuells. They were ordinarily very sickly, the Phisitians not knowing how to cure them being ignorāt of their sicknes.

some-

Foure sisters & a niece terribly tormented by the Diuels, are cured in Modena by his intercession.

fomerymes the Diuells caryed
them to high places, to caft
them downe headlong; and
other tymes to the moft re-
mot places of the houfe, when
fhutting the Dores they rent
theyr garments, pulled of the
haire from their heads beating
them, and cafting them to the
ground, with danger of their
liues : neither did they leaue
mifufing them in this manner
vntill thofe of the houfe, hearing the noife, came to help
them.

2.   All of them being ver
tuous women, brought vp in
the feare of God, and ve y mo-
deft in theyr words, they were
many tymes inforced by thofe
infernall beafts, to vtter vn-
feemely fpeaches, and horrible

blafphe-

blaſphemyes againſt God,
with ſuch terrible ſhoutes, as
amazed all that heard them.
They could not without great
violence apply themſelues to
prayer, nor ſay, nor heare any
word in the praiſe of God. It
was an intollerable thing for
them to be at Maſſe, and there
the Diuells made them ſound,
and fall to the ground, making outryes, & ſhouting with
ſuch violence, that they could
ſcarcely conteyne themſelues.
VVhen they went to confeſſion, they hindred them from
telling their ſinns, & bereaued
them of their forces, making
them to faynt, and cauſing
them to put out their tongues
after a foule manner, in mockery of the Holy Sacrament of

Con-

Confession, and of their Con-
fessours But that which tormented them most, were the
motions, and temptations of
the flesh, which continually
afflicted them. For they were
very honest women, and some
of them had dedicated their
virginity to God by vow. And
the Diuels themselues, com-
pelled by the exorcismes of the
Church, confessed, that their
intent was to depriue them of
their chastity, and to put them
in danger of loosing both their
spirituall, and corporal health:
but that they had laboured in
vayne by reason of the vse of
the Sacraments, with which
these good women defended
themselues, when they were
most of all afflicted.

3. Fur-

3 . Furthermore, these infernall spirits not being content to afflict them so many wayes, enraged with exceeding great fury, to see that weake women made them so great resistance, they killed the only sonne of the maryed sister, who was but 14. months old: & before they murthered him they threatned her, that they would kill him vpon such a certayne day, and so the child dyed at the tyme appointed, to the great griefe of his Mother, and of all the family. (How secret , and profound are the iudgments of our Lord !) These deuout, & afflicted women had taken all the spirituall remedies which they could imagine, to deliuer themselues

from

from this tyranny of the enemyes of mankynd They had
vsed Prayers, Masses Exorcismes, Holy water, Reliqaes
of Saynts, and other meanes
which the holy Church vseth.
They had byn a long tyme at
the directions of Priests & religions men of excellent vertue and prudence, that they
as good Phisitians might help,
and cure them. They had visited often the Holy house of
Loreto and other Sanctuaries
of great deuotion, and especially some in which our Lord
is wont more particulerly to
shew his power against the
Diuells, but nothing auailed,
because our Lord reserued
this occasion to glorify his
seruant Ignatius withall: by

whose

whose merits, and intercession they all foure, and the
niece also were deliuered from
the torments which they suffered : and had as good health,
and forces, with their disposition both inwardly and out-
wardly to their great contentment, as euer before. They
found themselues free from the
temptations of sensuality, and
from the difficulty in vocall, &
mentall prayer. They heard
Masse with great deuotion, &
cõfort. They liued with great
modesty, decency, and composition, and conuersed with
those of the house with great
affability, & sweetnes, as they
were wont, before they were
tormented by the Diuells;
which hath beene a matter of

great

great admiration to all that
were acquainted with them :
and much more by reason of
the manner with which our
Lord cured them, by the intercessiō of his Seruant Ignatius,
which was in this wise.

4. Father Rector of the Colledge of the Society of Iesus,
which is in the Citty of Modena, hauing vnderstood the
pittifull case of those poore
women, after he had throughly
considered, and commended it
to our Lord, by his instinct (as
the effect declared) went one
day to the house, carying with
him a picture of the B. Father,
which he kept for his deuotiō.
He entred into the roome
where the women were, at the
very tyme, that a Priest was

R   exor-

exorcising the Diuels; & without saying any thing, or telling any what he brought, he
put vp that picture of the Father vpon the wall, and betooke himself to prayer. Wher-
upon presently those helliish
spirits began to giue horrible
shouts, and to say, that it was
the picture of Ignatius Founder
of the Society, with which
they were grieuously tormented And withall they begā to
reuile at him egregiously, calling him bald, lame, & blynd:
& being pressed by the Priest
who exorcised them, to tel the
reason why they called him so:
they answered that they called him bald, because he had
not much hayre on his head
nor beard; and lame, because

his

his leggs were not of the same
length, one of them hauing
beene broken; and blynd, by
reason of his aboundance
of teares, wherby he had been
in great danger to loose his
fight: & they complayned, that
he came so farre, as Spayne, to
persecute them both in his life,
and after his death. And at the
same tyme many principall
Diuels departed with horrible
roarings from one of the sisters, leauing her almost dead,
and confessing the vertue of
Ignatius.

5. By this meanes the foresaid sisters, theyr mother, and
all the house conceyued great
deuotion towards the Blessed
Father, with hope by his intercession to obtayne the health

R 2   which

which they desyred ; and they
made a vow to obserue holy
all the dayes of their life, the
day of his death., and to fast
tha Eue. This deuotion increased with another new accident; for a Father of the Society called Augustine Viualdi,
being come at that tyme from
Rome to preach in Modena,
brought with him a reliquary,
in which among other ; he
had a relique of the B . Father,
which being placed secretly,
and without saying any thing
to any body, in the roome
where the sisters were , the
Diuels cryed out, saying: that
it was the Relique of Ignati.
telling from whence it came,
and who had brought it: confessing the intolerable tormét

which

which they suffered, and that
by his intercession they should
all be cast forth of those bodies. For God had determined
to glorify him in the world.

6. Another day a great
Diuell hauing mocked and
blasphemed at Ignatius before
his going out, being inforced
by God at the tyme of his departure, confessed to his great
confusion, that he was burnt
with that little peece of bone:
and he called him three tymes
a Saynt, saying : S. Ignatius,
S. Ignatius ; S. Ignatius casteth me forth by his humility
and patience, and by the deuotion, which he had to the
most Holy Virgin. Other
times, the Diuells desyring to
conceale that they were cast

out by the prayers of B. Ignatius, attributing that effect to
the vertue of other Saynts, to
whom the said sisters had particuler deuotion, at the tyme
of theyr going out, were inforced to cofesse the lye which
they had told, and to giue the
glory to Ignatius, saying that
God would serue himselfe of
him alone, in that occasion.

7. Other tymes with great
fury, at theyr departure, they
cryed out, saying: where is
thy might O Lucifer, since
that a peece of paper, with the
picture of this Priest casteth
vs forth, thou not being able
to make resistance? And many
tymes hauing beene exorcised
the whole day without profit,
they said, that they should ne-

uer depart, vnlesse Ignatius
were innocated, and called v-
pon, because God would haue
it so. And when the Priest said,
Impero vobis per merita B. Igna-
tij &c. I command you by the
merits of B. Ignatius &c they
presently went away with
great rage, and fury. Other
tymes they said: O God how
doest thou depriue vs of glory,
to giue it to this lame, & wrin-
kled Priest.

8. The same effects which
the Picture and Relique of the
Blessed Father had wrought,
were likewise caused by the
booke written of his life: for
it being caryed to the womens
house, for them to read vpon,
and layd vpon their head, or
breast, or some Chapter of his

life

life being read, the Diuels
were inforced to depart, and
to yeald themselues to the wil
of God, who is meruailous in
his Saynts, and giueth them
strength and vertue to tread
vpon Lyons, and to triumph
ouer al the powers of hel. This
battayle and contention, la-
sted for two months, at which
tyme the perfect victory was
obtayned. For as S. Bernard
saith, speaking of a Diuell,
which S. Malachy cast out of
two women; this delay was
not for want of power in the
Saynt, but by diuine dispen-
sation, that the presence of the
enemy, and the victory of the
Saynt, who cast them forth,
might be the better vnderstood.

Of the wonderfull force, and efi-
cacy of the words, & sayings
of B. Ignatius , in mouing
mens harts .

CHAP. XX.

HE had not only this do-
minion ouer the Diuels,
but also ouer the harts of
men , with whom he dealt .
For certainly the force which
our Lord gaue vnto his
words, were wonderfull, and
seemed more then humane ,
mouing mens harts, not with
the sweetnes, or elegacy of his
speach , but with the weight
of his spirit, and of the things
which he spake . He mol-
lified hard, and obstinate men

What
force
he had
to moue
mens
harts.

R 5 like

like wax, and altered them in
such sort, that they meruailed
at themselues; and at the
change, which they had
made. With two or three
words he often quieted, and
cured the infirme, and afflicted consciences and soules of
men, strengthing the weake,
and giuing them peace, and
security.

2. There was in our house
at Rome a Iew, called Isaac,
to be catechized, or instru-
cted, because he would become a Christian: He fell one
day into a great temptation,
and as one that were furious,
and besides himselfe, began
to say, that he would begone,
& would not be a Christian.
The holy Father commaun-

ded him to be brought before
him, and faid vnto him only
thefe words : *Stay with vs
Ifaac :* prefently he was quieted, and of a furious Lyon
became a gentle Lamb, and
remayned in the houfe, and
was baptized.

3. A brother called Iohn
Paul, who accompanyed our
Bleffed Father, was for a tyme
fo affaulted, and afflicted
with the Diuell, by an occafion of a certayne vayne, and
friuolous fcruple, that he
could not breath, nor find
any peace in his foule, eyther
by prayer, or pennances, or
the vfe of the holy Sacraméts,
or in any other thing which
he vfed for his remedy: fo that
he was fo fad, and melancho-

ly,

ly, that he seemed a lyuing
statua of death. He imparted
this his trouble to our Blessed
Father, who with only two
words, in answere, tooke a-
way, as with his hand, all
that perplexity, and agony,
and pulled vp the rootes of it
so perfectly, as if he had neuer
endured any such matter.

4. I knew another also
(whom I will not name be-
cause he is yet aliue) who being but a child, by reason of a
certaine fright, fel into so great
a feare, that he trembled at his
owne shaddow, and acquain-
ting our B. Father with that
passion, and vayne feare, he
with two words, that he
spake vnto him, restored him
to his former peace, and security.

rity . There happened two
other things to the same man,
which do very well declare
the efficacy, which God gaue
to the words of this his Seruant , and what force he had
to moue their harts, who treated with him . The one is ,
that being once very rebellious , and obstinate, in not following the wholsome coun-
sells which the Father gaue
him , with one only word ,
that he said vnto him , he was
in such sort changed , that he
began to cry out a loud , *I will
do it Father* , *I will doe it* . And
so he did, it seeming to him ,
that he had not power to do
otherwise , by reason of the
great motion, and impulsion ,
which he felt in his soule .

5. The

5. The other was that the same brother being tempted, and in a manner resolued not to perseuere in the Society, and making his generall Confession with the Blessed Father, with only these words, that he said vnto him , *I desire you, not to be vngratefull to one who hath done you so many fauours, as our Lord hath done*, he healed, quieted, and pacifyed him in such sort, that in that instant he determined to perseuere in his vocation : and hath deuoutly perseuered euer since, without hauing any the least trouble in this kind. And we might relate very many other things of this quality, by reason of which Father Francis Borgia, a man of such sanctity, and

pru-

prudence as is knowne, was wont to say, that B. Father Ignatius did speake, *tamquam potestatem habens*, as a man that had power, to imprint in mens harts what he would, and to moue them to what he would.

6. S. Bernard saith, that the holy Bishop S. Malachy tamed an vnruly, and very cholericke woman: & that in his opinion, this was a greater miracle, then if he had raysed one from death, because in the one miracle, he had raised the outward man and in the other the inward. This saith S. Bernard. But let vs follow the course of our narration, and declare some of the other miracles, which after the death

of

of the Blessed Father, our Lord hath wrought by his intercession, and especially these latter yeares, in which his Canonization hath byn treated of. For those which God hath done in diuers Prouinces, haue byn many, diuers, and great, to stirre vp the deuotion of the faithfull towards him, and to make him glorious vpon earth as he hath done in heauen.

Of the miraculous Cures of diseases, done by the intercession of B. F. Ignatius.

CHAP. XXI.

IN the very instant, that the Blessed Father gaue vp his Ghost, he appeared shyning,

and

At the instant in which he departed at Rome, he appeared to a Lady at Bononia.

and glorious , to a noble and
most deuout Matrone in Bononia , who was a widdow ,
called Margaret Dellio , and
greatly affected to the Society:
and he said vnto her ; *Margaret
I depart now , and I commend
the Society vnto you* . Hauing
said these words , he ceased to
appeare . And the pious woman related presently , what
she had seene to Father Francis
Palmius her Confessarius, and
the Rector of that Colledge ,
telling him , that without
doubt Father Ignatius was deceased, and that she had seene
him , describing him as liuely
as if she had knowne him before, whereas in truth she had
neuer seene him . And though
this were not held for certaine

S   when

when she related it, notwithstanding afterward, when the
newes of the Fathers death
came, and of the day, and
houre in which he went to a
better life, the thing was manifest.

2. The first day of Au-
guft in the yeare 1556. in
which the Father was buryed,
great multitudes of people
concured in Rome to his fune-
rall, to fee and reuerence him.
Among others which came,
there was a very deuout woman who bare affection to the
Society, called Bernardina,
and she had a daughter about
the age of 14. yeares, who was
molefted with a dangerous,
and troublefome infirmity of
the Lamperons, or Kings

He cu-
reth a
maid of
the
Kings
Euill.

Euill . And though she had spēt a good part of her wealth in curing her daughter , yet she could not get her health , but rather was euery day worse and worse . Her mother carryed her that day to the Church of the Society , with desire , that she might touch the holy Fathers body , and commend her selfe vnto him , and by his intercessiō obtaine of our Lord her health, which the Phisitians could not procure . But the throng was so great , that how much soeuer the mother , and daughter endeauored , they could not by any meanes come where the F. body lay. Seing their desire thus frustrate, they requested to haue something that had

touched the B. Fathers body,
and the mother with great deuotion and faith, applyed it to
her daughters neck, touching
with it the Lamperons, and
fores, which were in a manner
feftered: and by the mercy of
our Lord, and the merits of
his feruant Ignatius, the mayd
was perfectly cured, to the admiration of all thofe that
heard of it, and acknowledg-
ment of the Fathers fanctity,
who after his death gaue health to thofe, which hartily
commended themfelues vnto
him.

3. In the yeares 1569.
vpon the 31. of Iuly (which
was the day of his deceafe) the
body of the Bleffed Father was
tranflated the firft tyme, and

*Muſick
hard in
his tòbe.*

there

there was heard by a certaine
deuout feruant of God for the
fpace of two dayes, moft fweet
muficke and harmony , as it
were of voices , in his Sepul-
cher .

4. In Rome a Lady called
Drufilla Turfellina being very
much vexed with a vehement
feuer, and with the head-ach ,
hauing vfed many remedyes,
& byn let bloud in her armes,
noftrills , and head , without
profit , her ficknes rather in-
creafing euery day ; was prefently healed by a relique of
one of the Bleffed Fathers bones , layd vpon her forehead .

5. Another woman na-
med Olimpia Norina had fuch
a vehement payne in her eyes,
that fhe came to loofe her fight,

*He cu-
reth a
burning
feuer.*

He giueth sight to a blind woman

and for the space of three moneths had such a continuall ague, and payne in her head, that she could not rest. They brought her a subscription of the Blessed Fathers hand, at the tyme that her payne was at the greatest, laying it vpon her forehead, and eyes, and she began to see, and was ryd of her ague and payne.

6. In the same Citty in the yeare 1597. a noble mans child of seauen yeares old, called Hierome Gabriell, being sick of a pestilent feuer (called a Tauerdillo) and of a plurify;

He restoreth health to a child in a māner past recouery.

hauing also the wormes, so that there was litle hope of his life, was healed with the same subscription of the Blessed Father.

7. In

7. In the yeare 1599. Lady Ioane Vrsina, being but a child, daughter to Cornelia Vrsina Dutchesse of Cesi, had so great a cough, that she could scarsely breath, or suck. The Dutches her mother commended her very earnestly and deuoutly to Blessed Father Ignatius, and beseeched him to obtayne the health of her daughter: wherupō the child hauing byn a night and a halfe without rest, presently fell a sleepe, and her cough ceased, and she began to sucke her Nurses breast. For which cause the Dutches cōmaunded a Tablet to be set on the Fathers graue in remembrance of the fauour, which she had receiued.

8. In the same yeare 1599

He deliuereth another child from a dangerous cough & shortnes of breath.

S 4 Angela

He re-
storeth
hearing
to a
deafe
woman.

Angela Ruggiera was trou-
bled with an extraordinary
noise in her head for almoſt a
yeare, and loſt the hearing of
her right eare; wherto applying a relique of the Bleſſed Father, and making a vow to
faſt with bread and water the
day of his departure, and to
communicate the day following, recouered perfect health,
and remayned free from that
infirmity.

9. In the ſame yeare 1599.
vpon a monday, being the 19.
of Iuly Father Michael Vazques a profeſſed Father of the
Society of Ieſus, and Prefect of
the ſtudyes in the Roman
Colledge, had ſuch a terrible fit of the cholicke, & ſtone,
that being in a cold ſweat, and

He fre-
eth one
from a
vehe-
ment fit
of the
ſtone.

as

as it were in an agony, and
without feeling, seemed ready
to giue vp the ghost. They applyed many remedyes to ease
his payne, but all without profit: yea it seemed that his payn
increased by the multiplying
of remedyes. He desired them
to bring him a Relique of B.
Father Ignatius, which they
did, and he tooke it with great
deuotion, and commending
himself very deuoutly to his
Holy Father, he put it to
the part where his payne was
most sharp and vehement: and
presently the payne ceased in
that part, but remayned in o-
thers, which likewise afflicted
him much. But laying the sacred Relique vpon those also,
the payne seemed to fly from

S 5 before

before it, so that at length he remayned altogether whole & free.

10. And foure or fiue houres after he began to cast forth without any payne many peeces of the stone, imbrued with bloud, and as it were enwrapped in little peeces of flesh; the Phisitians iudging, that the stone was dissolued by the vertue of that Relique, and bebecause it was sharp, had torne the passages. Forthwith the sick Father rose out of his bed, against the opinion of many, because he iudged that health not to be humane, but from Heauen, and obtayned by the merits of the B. Father, & consequently that it would be perfect, and that he had no cause

to feare. The said Father Michael Vazques had at that
tyme the care to deale with the
Cardinalls of the Congrega-
tion of holy Rites, or Ceremo-
nies, concerning the Canonization of the B. Father, and it
seemed, that our Lord sent him
that so suddaine, and sharp a
sicknes, that hauing had experience of the Blessed Fathers
fauour in his owne person, he
might be the more earnest
in procuring his Canoni-
zation .

11. The same yeare 1599. a
godly Matron of Rome, ha-
uing a canker in one of her
breasts, and by the iudgment
of Phisitians being so far gone,
that it seemed she would short-
ly dye; making her prayers, at

the

He cu-
reth a
canker.

the B. Fathers tomb, she began presently to feele the benefit of his intercession, and without any other corporall medicine, she became well within few dayes : for which cause her husband caused an Hearse of cloth of siluer to be layd vpon his tomb, and the woman her selfe sent the portrature of a breast made of siluer and gilt, in remembrance of the benefit receyued .

12. Another called Orinthia Casali, being with child, and without hope of life, because the said child was dead in her body, applying a subscription of the Blessed Father therto, was deliuered of the dead childe, the mother her self remayning in good health.

He deliuereth a woman of a dead child.

13. Let

13. Let vs omit the other miracles which God hath wrought in Rome (being many) and let vs come to other Prouinces of Italy . In the Marca of Ancona is scituated the Sacred House of our Lady of Loreto, in which the most Holy Virgin was borne, and the Eternal Word clothed himselfe with our flesh . In this place a child of six yeares old , fell into so grieuous a sicknes, that the Phisitians gaue him ouer . They laid a litle peece of B. Father Ignatius his garment vpon him , commending him to his prayers, and presently he began to be better, and was perfectly cured .

A child past cure recouered.

14. In the Citty of Recanati, which is about 3 . miles from Loreto,

He healeth diuers diseases.

Loreto, the yeare 1599. a woman much troubled with an
ague, and payne in her ftomake, commending her felf to
the Bleſſed Father, was freed
from both. And a youth being
in danger of his life, by bleeding at his noſe ſo aboundan-
tly that it could not be ſtaun-
ched, hauing a Relique of the
Bleſſed Father applyed, left
bleeding. And another wo-
man, which had a great payne
in her breaſts, there being an
impoſtume bred in them, the
impoſtume did breake by vertue of the ſame Relique.

15.   In the ſame Citty a
Gétlemã named Horatius Leo-
pardus, being in the moneth
of October of the ſame yeare
1599. in danger of his life by

a

a fit of the ſtone, & retentiõ of
vrine, not finding any remedy,
he commended himſelfe very
affectuouſly to our B. Lady,
beſeeching her by the merits
of B. Father Ignatius to heale
him, and deſyring the Father
himſelfe to be his good aduocate. At that very inſtant his
payne was eaſed, and he began to make water; and afterward, he caſt forth much gra-
uell, and ſtones, broken in
litle peeces, and ſo remayned
altogether free.

16. Heere alſo the ſame
yeare & moneth, a Lady called
Lucandia, wife to Pompeius
Georgij, hauing beene very
ſick for the ſpace of fiue
monthes, and endured great
paynes, and palpitations of

He cu-
reth
paynes
of the
hart.

her

her hart, applying vnto it a little peece of the Fathers garment, prefently found herfelf well. And the fame woman hauing gone with child nyne moneths, and caft out of her body twéty pounds of bloud, being therewith much weakned, and in a manner without fenfe, fhe earnefty commended her felf to the B. Father, &

that bloudy flux ceafed, and fhe came to her felfe: and afterward being much opprefled with the paynes of childbearing, not being able to be deliuered, fhe was brought to bed of a dead fonne without payne, fhe herfelfe remayning in life, and health, commending her felfe to the B. Father.

17. In the Citty of Macerata, which is about three leagues from Loreto, Bleſſed Father Ignatius appeared to a woman called Elizabeth Morena, Niece to the Lord Biſhop of the ſame Citty, ſhe being like to dye, and without hope of life, in the moneth of Nouēber of the yeare 1599. & taking her by the hãd, he tould her, that ſhe ſhould ere long be reſtored to perfect health, willing her to riſe, and giue thankes to god for the mercy which he vſed towards her.

18. In the Citty of Naples, in the moneth of Iune of the yeare 1599. Doña Ioana of Aragon, Princeſſe of Beltran, and Dutcheſſe of Terra-noua, had a great payne, &

He appeareth to a ſick woman, reſtoring her health.

T ſwel-

He deli-
uereth a
Lady.
from a
paine &
ſwelling
in her
breſt.

ſwelling in her right breaſt:
& finding no remedy, amõgſt
many which were applyed in
the ſpace of foure moneths,
omitting them all, as vnpro-
fitable, and laying vpon her
breaſt, with much deuotion,
the picture of the B. Father,
ſhe became well the ſame
day: and comming to Rome
this laſt Holy yeare of 1600,
commaunded a Tablet of ſil-
uer, with foure great waxe
Tapers to be ſet vpon the B.
Fathers tomb, on Eaſter day,
in thankes giuing.

19. In the Citty of Nola,
the yeare 1599. in the moneth
of Nouember, a knight named
Francis Blaſius, being much
vexed with a peſtilét ague, &
with a grieuous payne in his

head

head and ftomack, fo that in the iudgmēt of the Phifitians, he was in danger of his life. His mother Zenobia Tolphia exhorted him to lay a Relique of the bone of B. Father Igna-tius to his head, & commend himfelfe vnto him, defyring his fauour. He did fo, and re-mayned free from all his paynes, and his whole ficknes.

20. In the Citty of Lecha (which is in the Prouince of Apulia, in the Kingdome of Naples) the yeare 1594. a wo-man called Patientia, feruant to a Lady named Antonina Cubella, had fuch a terrible payne in her fide, that it was accounted incurable, in fo much, that they prepared her graue. They brought her a

A womā cured from a payne in her fide.

T 2 Relique

Relique of the Blessed Father
Ignatius, and presently she fell
a sleep (which she could not
do before) and in her sleep,
the Father appeared vnto her,
in priestly attyre, & sayd vnto
her: Daughter, commend thy
self to God, and he will heale
thee: vpon hearing of which
wordes, she found her self free
from her payne.

21. In the same Citty of
Lecha a child of three yeares
old, sonne to the Baron of Be-
gli-boni, fell from his Nurses
armes vpon the ground, & did
notably hurt his right knee,
which grew euery day worse,
because the Nurse for feare
concealed the fal. And it went
so far that it was necessary to
open the childs knee oftener

then

A child
healed
of a
wound
in his
knee.

then once, and yet this helped
not: wherfore comming to cut
it the third tyme, the Father
fearing his Sonnes death,
(whome he did see consumed
with the wound, and with the
ague which followed thereupon) went to the Colledge of
the Society, & there they gaue
him a Relique of the B. Fathers
bone; which he layd vpon the
child, before they opened his
knee the third tyme, and when
the Surgeons came to do it,
they found him much better,
and within a few dayes altogeather well.

22. A Father of the Society,
called Natalis Masuca, sayling
to Sicily, was taken by the
Turkes, and afterward a great
storme arose, in which he ex-

A Fathe
deliue-
redfron
a tépeſt
and cap
tiuity.

T 3   pected

pected to be drowned. He commended himself to B. Father Ignatius, and heard presently a voyce, which said vnto him. *Doubt not, for thou shalt not be drowned in this tempest, nor be caryed into Turky.* The storme ceased, and the Turkes ship was taken by the Christians, neere to the Ile Lampadosa, & so he was deliuered both from the sea, and the Pyrats.

23.   In the Citty of Palermo, a child of three yeares old called Cosmus Ferier, sonne to a famous Phisitian, had such a terrible ague, & loosnesse of his body, that his Father himselfe hauing giuen him ouer, prepared all things necessary for his buriall; but hauing layd vpon him a peece of a vestiment,

A child cured of in ague, & loosenesse.

ment, in which Bleſſed Father
Ignatius had ſaid Maſſe, he
forthwith began to be much
better, and the ſame day recouered his health to the great
admiration, and ioy of his
Father, and thoſe of the houſe.
Now let vs come to Spayne.

Of diuers Miracles wrought in
Spaine, by the interceſsion
of B.F. Ignatius.

CHAP. XXII.

IN the yeare 1570 or 1571.
in the City of Toledo, one
day in winter, a little before
night, an ancient woman,
called Vega, ſeruant to Alonſo
of Villa-Real Duron, and of
Mary de Torres his wife, fell

He deli
uereth
woman
from a
payne i
her ſid

T 4   into

into an exceeding payne of her
fide, which was fo vehement,
that the Philitiás willed her to
côfeffe, & receiue the moft B.
Sacramēt, & make her laft wil
& teftament the fame night,
fearing that fhe would not
lyue till morning: a deuout &
vertuous, man called Iohn of
Mefa, friend to the faid Alonfo
of Villa-Real, vnderftanding
this, hauing firft betaken himfelfe to prayer, layd vpon that
fyde of the ficke womē where
the payne was, a little peece of
a lynnen cap, and another of a
lether ftomacher, which B.
Father Ignatius was wont to
vfe, and the faid Iohn of Mefa
caryed about him for his deuotion: & at the very inftant,
that he did this, the fick wo-

man became whole, and well,
saying: *O Maister Iohn of Mesa,
what haue you done to me, that
you haue taken away my payne,
and sicknes?*

2. In the Citty of Burgos,
Doña Francisca of Beruy, a
professed Nunne in the monastery of S. Dorothy, of great
recollection, and vertue, being very much tormented
with the cholick, and stone,
hauing recourse to the intercession of the said Blessed Father, in the space of one yeare
little more or lesse, came to cast
forth, more then an hundreth
stones, little, and great, in a
manner without any payne at
all. And in the yeare 1593.
hauing broken a veyne in her
breast, not being able to

He cu-
reth the
colicke
stone,
& blee-
ding.

T 5   staunch

staunch the bloud, which she
cast out of her mouth, laying
vpon her breast a little peece
of the first sackcloth, which
the Blessed Father clad himselfe withall in Montserat,
when he gaue his apparell to
the poore man, the bloud presently ceased, and stayed.

3. There was in the Con-
uent of the Nunnes, commõ-
ly called Huelgas, one named
Doña Ioanna of Gongora,
very sickly, in so much, that
she had procured a Breue of
his Holynes, that she might
go out of her Monastery to
take Phisick: but commen-
ding her selfe to the Holy Father, and keeping his picture
in her Cell, she remayned so
free, and sound, that she stood

He cu-
reth o-
ther in-
firmi-
ties.

no

no more in need of leaue to go abroad for her health .

4. Another deuout woman of the order of S . Francis, named Mary of Auala , who was much afflicted in spirit , had counsell to commend her selfe to Blessed Father Ignatins , that by his meanes , she might obtayne ease, & remedy of her trouble: and she betaking her selfe to prayer , forgot the name of Ignatius , and sayd : *O Saynt Athanasius, help me in the fight of our Lord , that he will be pleased to deliuer me from this great temptation , and affliction which I endure .* When she said these wordes , she heard a voice, that answered : *He is not called Athanasius, but Ignatius: & doubt*

not

He helpeth the trouble of the mind.

not, *but that by his intercession,*
thou shalt obtaine that, which
thou desyrest of our Lord: as indeed she did.

5. Another man named
Lancelot Ruffin of Flanders
being sick of a pestilent ague,
and giuen ouer by the Phisitians, by the meanes of a subscription of the B. Father, recouered perfect health, and
rose vp sound, and well, to
the admiration of the Phisitians, & of all those that knew
his danger.

6. The same happened to
to Don Lopez of Castro,
nephew to Doña Eleano-
ra Gallo, who at that tyme
was Abbesse of the Mona-
stery of S. Dorothy, who
being giuen ouer by all the

Phisi-

He cureth a dangerous feuer.

Phisitians which had him in hand, afwell by thofe who liued in Burgos, as by others whome he had fent for from Valliadolid, comméding himfelfe to Father Ignatius, & promifing to giue a certayne almes in his name, was prefently healed, & deliuered of his infirmity.

7. A religious, and graue Father of the order of Saynt Auguftine, belonging to the Conuent of the Citty of Burgos, being in Quintanilla of Somuñon a Town within the Archbifhoprick of Burgos, whither he went, moued by charity, to adminifter the Sacraments to thofe who were fick of the plague: vpon the eleuenth of Nouember in the

A maid infected with the plague is healed with the Fathers picture

yeare 1599. heard the confeſſion of a yong woman about
22. yeares old, called Mary,
daughter to Iohn Gomez huſ-
bandman, who was ſick of a
ſtrong ague, & infected with
the plague, he gaue her counſell to commend her ſelf very
earneſtly to Bleſſed Father Ignatius. and he gaue her a picture of the ſame Father, to
put in her boſome;& with this
only remedy, within an houre
after he found her without
eyther ſoare, or ague.

8· Many that were infe-
cted with the plague, in the
Citty of Burgos, drinking
of the water, in which a
bone of Bleſſed Father Ignatius had beene dipped, and
commending themſelues to

him,

Many
that had
the
plague
recouer
by drin-
king of
the wa-
ter in
which
one of
the Fa-
thers
bones
had byn
dipped.

him, recouered perfect health.
And Francis Ortiz Curate, &
Paſtour of S. Peter and S. Felix auoucheth, that many were
ſo healed, and that he gaue
them the water. For when humane remedyes fayled, he betooke himſelf to diuyne, and
that this was publick in the
Citty.

9. The ſame is teſtifyed
by Bachelour Sanchius of Can-
tabrana, Curate, and Paſtour
of the Church of S. Stephen,
to haue happened to himſelfe,
being infected with the plague,
and hauing a great and vehement tertian feuer, & that
taking of the foreſaid water,
and commending himſelfe to
Father Ignatius, he was healed.
And Abel de-la-Torre, Cu_

rate,

rate, and Paſtour of S. Mar-
tyns, in the ſame Citty of Burgos, being infected with the
plague, drinking of the ſaid
water, which his mother
brought him, at the ſame inſtant that he tooke it, felt
himſelfe well, and was freed
from his ague.

10. Francis Ortez afore-
ſaid, Curate, and Paſtour of
the Church of S. Peter and S.
Felix in the ſame Citty of Burgos, hauing endured by the
ſpace of fyue yeares a great infirmity of certayne humors in
his knees, and ankles, with
much payne and trouble, by
cōmending himſelfe to the B.
Father, was healed, neuer feeling that infirmity afterward.

11. In the Citty of Ma-

drid

He hel-
peth one
from a
lamneſſe
in his
knees.

drid Father Michael Garſes, a profeſſed Father of the Society of Ieſus, had a rhewme that fell into his right eye, and did put him to ſuch exceſſiue payne, that he could fynd no eaſe, eyther in letting bloud, or in any remedy which was vſed: but rather the payne ſeemed to increaſe by the multiplying of remedyes, ſo that he could not take any reſt day or night. Finally the ninth of September in the yeare 1596. hauing endured a moſt vehement payne in his ſaid eye, vntill ſeauen of the clock at night, Father Bartholomew Perez, who is at this day Aſſiſtant of the Society at Rome, taking compaſſion of him, gaue him a ſubſcription of B. Father Ig-

He ſuddenly taketh away a vehemēt payne of the eyes with his ſubſcription.

V   natiuʒ

natius his hand, and willed
him to commed himselfe vnto
him, and tolay it vnto his eye:
for he hoped that he would
deliuer him from that payne,
as he had done othres who had
commended themselues vnto
him. Father Garſes kneeled
downe, betaking himſelfe to
prayer, and layd the ſubſcription vnto his eye, when his
payne was at the greateſt;
which preſently was taken a-
way, and a little after he went
to bed, and ſlept all that night
with good repoſe, and the
next morning heard confeſ-
ſions in the Church: and we
of the houſe did ſee his eye
weil, which we had ſeene the
day before very bloudy, and
full of water.

12. In Gandia a maide of
13. yeares old, called Francis
Vinoles, had byn ill at eafe for
the fpace almoſt of a yeare, of
a great payne in one of her
leggs, which made her halt,
& did put her to much payne,
eſpecially when the weather
was cold, which was very
contrary to her diſeaſe. This
mayd the day of the Circum-
ciſion of our Lord, in the yeare
1600. went to Maſſe (not
without great difficulty) becauſe it was ſo great a day, and
returned home much afflicted,
by reaſon of the payne which
greatly tormented her. Her
mother willed her to cōmend
herſelf earneſtly to bleſſed Father Ignatius, and layd one of
his ſubſcriptions vpon her:

He hea-
leth a
lame
woman.

V 2 and

and in that very inſtant the
ſick maid felt her ſelfe perfectly well , and free from that
payne : and began to go , as if
ſhe neuer had any . Her Father
(who was a Phiſitian) and all
the houſe accounted it a miracle : and in ſigne of thank-
fulnes, preſently the day following , the mayd , and her mother came to the Church of
the Society of Ieſus , to render
thankes to our Lord , and to
his great Seruant Ignatius ,
preſenting him with a picture
of wax .

13. Like to this miracle is
another , which happened in
the moneth of October in the
yeare 1600. in the ſame Citty
of Gandia , to Ioſepha Borgia
wife to Gaſpar Harrera . For

the

the said Iosepha, not being able for the space of more then a moneth, scarse to moue her selfe, by reason of an exceeding great payne in her knee, and finding no remedy by any medicine, she began to commend her selfe to the Blessed Father, with great deuotion, and to say fiue tymes the *Pater noster*, and *Aue Maria*. And hauing done this for three dayes, being one night in her bed, and commending her selfe vnto him with many teares (because she felt her selfe much tormented with that payne) she presently reposed, & slept, and in her sleepe the Blessed Father appeared vnto her, and with a serene, and cherefull countenance told her, that he

V 3 came

came to cure her, & touching her knee with his blessed hand, he freed her from al that payne, and she awaking found her selfe perfectly well, and presently the next morning came to the Church of the Society, and brought a picture of wax in testimony, and remembrance of the fauour receyued at our Lords hands.

14. But yet more notable is that which happened in the same Citty, in the moneth of Nouember following, to a recollected Virgin of the age of 40. yeares, called Iosepha Castella, who was sick of the goute, which was wont to take her with such great force, and violence, that it depriued her of her iudgment, and many

He cureth the Gout.

people

people could scarse hold her
from hurting, and beating her
selfe: and when she was out
of this fit, she remayned with
such a terrible payne of her
hart, and so great affliction of
mynd, her body also being so
wearied, and broken, that for
all that day, and the day following, she could not moue her
selfe, nor do any thing. But
hauing vnderstood of the fauours, which our Lord did in
this tyme in diuers places by
the intercession of the Blessed
Father; one night when her
disease had assayled her more
fiercely and violently, then
at other tymes, comming a
litle to her self, she comended
her selfe, as earnestly as she
could, to the Blessed Father

with great confidence, saying
fiue tymes the *Pater noster*, and
the *Aue Maria*, and presently
in the same instant, she found
her selfe altogeather well, and
as sound, and free from that
sadnes, and payne of her hart,
and from the other accidents
with which she had remained
all that tyme, as she was wont
at other tymes before. She
slept, and reposed that night
very well (which she could
not do at other tymes, when
she had those fits)and presently so soone as it was day, she
rose out of her bed, whereat
her sister, and brother-in-law
meruailed to see her goe vp
and downe the house. She bad
them not wonder, but giue
thankes to our Lord, who by

meanes

meanes of B . Father Ignatius
had giuen her moſt perfect
health , ſo that ſhe had not ſo
much as any ſigne of her ſicknes . After eight , or tenne
dayes , the ſame mayd fell into
ſuch an extreme fit of the
Cholicke , that ſhe expected
death: and with the deuotion,
which ſhe had conceiued towards the Bleſſed Father , ſhe
commended her ſelfe to him ,
and preſently remayned altogeather free from that payne
alſo. And in token of acknow-
ledgment , ſhe came to the
Church of the Society , and
brought two pictures of wax,
all that were preſent concur-
ring with her in prayſing our
Lord .

15 . We may add to theſe

Alſo the cholike.

V 5   miracles

miracles another, which God
hath wrought in the same Citty of late, vpon the 12. of De-
cember of this last yeare 1600.
A Girle of 7. yeares old was so
sick of an ague, and a swelling
in her face, that for two dayes,
and two nights she could take
no rest, nor drinke so much as
one drop of water, so that her
parés thought rather of burying her, then of curing her.
One of the childs Aunts saw
by chance a picture of Blessed
Father Ignatius, which had
byn brought to her Father,
that he might set it in a frame
(for he was a ioyner) she tooke
it, and layd it vpon the sick
childs head, with great confidence, bidding her commend
her selfe to that Saint, and to

make

A child
healed
of an A-
gue and
sweel-
ling in
the face.

make a vow , that she would performe some deuotion towards him for nyne dayes togeather, if she recouered. Within a quarter of an houre, the child called her mother , and told her , that she was found and well , and that the holy Father Ignatius had healed her , desiring her to giue her some thing to eate. She did eate, drink , and sleepe that night, as one that was perfectly well; and forthwith the day following , she and her Aunt went to the Colledge of the Society , to giue our Lord thankes , and began to performe the deuotion promised , and presented a picture of wax .

Of

*Of diuers other Miracles of B.
F. Ignatius, done in other
parts of the world.*

CHAP. XXIII.

NOvv let vs paſſe to the
Iland, and Citty of Ma-
jorca, in which our Lord hath
wrought great wonders theſe
yeares paſt, by the interceſſion
of Bleſſed Father Ignatius.
Ioane Claray Noguera, a vertuous, and exemplar widdow
being very ill of her eyes, and
hauing loſt the ſight firſt of
her right eye, and afterward of
her left, applying a ſubſcription of Bleſſed Father Ignatius
his hand vnto them, was ſo
perfectly healed, that preſent-

A wid-
dow re-
ſtored
to her
ſight.

ly

ly the day following she could worke with her needle, and fixe her eyes as stedfastly vpon her worke, as before she was blind .

2 . Another Lady called N. Sureda, wife to George Sureda who being in exceeding great payne of child-bearing, and could not be deliuered in many dayes ; with the subscription of the Blessed Father brought forth a sonne safe and sound , the mother also hauing her health , and receyuing great contentment , and ioy , as all the rest of that family likewise did .

He helpeth many women in their labour of child-bearing.

3 . This also happened more notably to another woman, wife to Saluador Mereader, who hauing wholy lost her

forces

forces, so that she could not be
deliuered : and fearing least
her child were dead, by the
same subscription recouered
her courage, and strength,
and brought forth a sonne, to
whome at his baptisme they
gaue the name of Ignatius, because he was borne by his intercession.

4. Magdalen Suau wife to
Peter Suau, endured for three
dayes most terrible paynes of
child-bearing, and vpon S.
Laurence his day, in the yeare
1598. the subscription which
we haue mentioned of the
Blessed Father, being brought
vnto her, whilest she was in
that distresse in her bed, she
rose out of it, and after a new
manner, all that were present

calling

calling vpon the name of Bleffed Ignatius, fhe was deliuered
of a child, hauing his head gro-
wing betwixt his leggs. And
yet our Lord vouchfafed to
preferue the mother, who was
very faynt and weake, without any hurt or harme; the
child alfo being fayre, and in
good health, which caufed all
the ftanders by to praife our
Lord, for the wayes which he
taketh to honour his Saints.
With thefe, and other like accidents the fame of the fauour
which God our Lord doth
to women in childbirth, by the
merits of Father Ignatius was
fo fpread abroad, that both
poore, and rich, when they
found themfelues in that danger, did take him for their ad-

uocate

uocate, and vse his subscription, by which meanes they
found remedy, and reliefe in
their necessities.

5. Another woman, called
Ieronyma Rebaça, was many
dayes in danger of her life, by
reason of the great, and terrible paynes, which she suffered
in child-bearing, being also exceeding weake and faynt, and
hauing vsed many remedyes
without profit, thinking that
the child was dead (becaufe it
moued not) they would haue
giuen her a certayne strong
medicine, to make her voyd
it forth, though not without
much danger of her owne life.
But she insteed of that dangerous potion, betooke herfelf to the remedyes from heauen,

uen , and defired to haue the fubfcription of Bleffed Father Ignatius brought vnto her, by which God did worke fo many , and fo great wonders in Majorca. They brought it to her vpon the 20. of October of the fame yeare 1598 . and within halfe a quarter of an houre fhe was deliuered of a fonne , being aliue , and in good health . And that which caufed moft admiration was , that the child had his mouth full of the potions , which the mother had taken three dayes before . The midwife tooke them out of his mouth, and the child prefently cryed , which made all the reft to laugh for ioy .

6 . One of the women ,

X   which

He hea-
leth a
woman
of a
paine,
with
which
she had
beene
trou-
bled 16.
yeares.

which was present at this miracle, was Ieronyma Pỳ, wife
to Raphaell Pỳ, who for six-
teene yeares had endured most
vehement, & continuall payne
in her iawes, not hauing found
any remedy which could mi-
tigate the same, and togeather
with this, she was troubled
with a loose tooth, which caused her much payne when she
did eate. This woman hauing
seene what God had wrought
in that deliuery of Ieronyma
Rebaça, moued with deuo-
tion; desired to haue the said
subscription of the Blessed Father, which she kissed, and
reuerenced; and presently in
that instant, she was deliuered
from her paynes, and the loose
tooth also, became as fast as

any

any of the rest.

7. This good woman, & her husband were so thankful, and deuout to Blessed Father Ignatius, that they deserued to receaue, another greater benefit at our Lords hand, by his intercession. For the day following, being the 21. of October, a sonne of theirs called Iohn Pỳ, fell sick of so terrible, and dangerous a double tertian ague, that hauing confessed, and receyued, he lost his iudgment the fourth day, his toung was thicke, his eyes holow and cloudy, togeather with the other accidents and signes of death. Vpon the 19. of October, they laid the subscription of the Blessed Father vpon him, beseeching our

One cured being in danger of death

X 2 Lord

Lord with much deuotion, & teares to graunt the ficke man his health. And at that very inftant the ague was quite taken away, & he recouered his iudgment and fpeach, and his eyes became cleare. And this being at eight of the clock at night, forthwith the day following in the morning he rofe out of his bed found and well, and the Phifitian comming at that houre to vifit him (thinking that he would be either dead, or in his laft agony) he found him walking, without any figne of his ague, or former ficknes.

8. By chaunce a horfe ran ouer a Surgeon called Bartholomew Conftantius, and bruized him fo forely, that his head

seemed

seemed to be frozen, and he had so great a payne in his eyes that he could not take any rest eyther day, or night. He lost the sight of one of his eyes, & the other remayned so weake and tender, that he could not endure any glimpse of light. The Phisitians had giuen him ouer for incurable, and vpon Holy Wednesday in the morning, the yeare 1599. he desired with singuler deuotion to haue the subscription of the Blessed Father. At the tyme that they brought it, and it came into the chamber where he was, before they gaue it him, that great cold in his head, and the vehement payne in his eyes ceased, & he found both in body, and spirit an ex-

X 3   traor-

traordinary comfort. Hauing
feene the meruailous effects of
that fubfcription, he prefently
tooke from his head the ker-
chers, and caps, which he
had to defend it from the cold
that he endured, and he
cryed out, faying : *I am now*
well, and found, and without
payne eyther of eyes, or head.
Whereupon he commaunded
the dores, and windowes of
his chamber to be opened,
(which before he had kept
fhut to keep out the light) and
the day following being foûd
and cheerefull, he went to the
Colledge of the Society, to
praife our Lord, for hauing deliuered him by the interceffion
of the B. Father, and to relate
what had happened vnto him.

9. A

9. A woman called Co-
lonia Vich, wife to Lewes
Vich, hauing endured a moſt
vehement headach three moneths, and finally loſt the ſight
of one of her eyes, the lyd
therof falling downe and co-
uering it, ſo that the Surgeons
could by no meanes lift it vp
againe, and thereupon gaue
her ouer as incurable. They
brought her the ſubſcription
vpon the fift of May, and in
the very inſtant, that they layd
it vpon her ſore eye, calling
vpon the name of the Bleſſed
Father, the lyd was preſently
lifted vp of it ſelfe, and ſhe recouered her ſight, and went to
the Colledge of the Society,
to giue praiſe to our Lord.

10. Let vs not forget Ger-

He deli-
uereth a
woman
from
danger
of death
in child-
bearing.

many, where in a Towne called Ebelperge, not far from
the Citty of Monachium (in
which the Dukes of Bauaria
reside) a woman being in terrible paynes of child-bearing,
and hauing continued two
dayes, and two nights in labour, with great affliction
and anxiety, not being able
to be deliuered, the third day
fhe found her felf fo faynt,
& without ftrength, that fhe
feemed more likely to dye, thē
otherwife. Her Husband being very much afflicted, went
to a Father of the Society, who
was there, crauing his aduife
and help in that tribulation.
The Father remembring the
Miracles, which our Lord
wrought in many places, by
the

the interceſſion of B. Father
Ignatius, eſpecially with women who were in Danger
by child-bearing, kneeling
downe, beſeeched the Bleſſed
Father with great deuotion to
fauour that poore woman in
ſuch extreme neceſſity. And
becauſe he had no other Relique of the Father to ſend her,
he tooke the rules which the
ſame B. Father had written for
the Society, with much deuotion, and many teares, and in-
foulding, and bynding them
vp in a paper, he gaue them to
the womans husband, that he
might lay them vpon her, as a
ſacred thing, willing him not
to doubt, but that God would
fauour her. He did ſo, and the
woman preſently recouered

X 5 ſtrength,

strength, & within fiue houres was deliuered of a son, strangly wrapped vp in a thinne skin, to the great admiratió of the Midwife and other womé of experience, and both the sonne, and the mother lyued.

He procureth another happy deliuery.

11.   In Hungary in the Towne called Turroz, the yeare 1594. a woman hauing béene 3. dayes, in very terrible paynes of child-birth, and in feare both of her owne, and her childs death, with a Relique of the B. Father, was forthwith deliuered of a son; she remaying in perfect health, and yealding thankes vnto our Lord.

12.   Let vs not passe in silence, what our Lord hath wrought in the Indies (though

they

they be far from vs.) In the
yeare 1598. in the moneth of
September, a little ſhip, called *Sancta Maria de Regla*, departed out of the hauen of the
Bleſſed Trinity (which is in
the Iland of Cuba) towards
the Citty of Carthagena : in
which with don Bartholomeo
Lobo-Guerrero, Archbiſhop
of the new Kingdome of Granada, there went at his requeſt
and in his company, the Father Alphonſus Medranus, &
Francis Figueroa of the Society of Ieſus, with other
Prieſts, and Laymen. Sayling
thus, and comming within
ſight of Iamayca, vpon the 23.
of September, they were aſ-
ſayled with ſuch a terrible, and
fearefull ſtorme, that they all

accoun-

accounted themselues loft mē.
For both the great and fore
mafts of the fhip were broken,
& their fayles torne in peeces,
and the wind fo furious , that
they could not fet vp any
other, and the waues of the fea
entered into the fhip, with
fuch violence, that it rather
feemed to fayle vnder, then a-
boue the water . The Pilot,
called Domingo Rodriguez
did let it run at all aduentures
thinking that it was paft all
humane remedy, if God did
not fend them fome from Heauen .The tempeft hauing endured thus one whole day , &
waxing euery houre greater ,
the paffengers made their re-
courfe to our Lord imploring
his Diuine help . The Fathers

of

of the Society calling to mynd
the miracles , which our Lord
did at that tyme by the inuocation of their Bleſſed Father
Ignatius , commended themſelues vnto him,with great affect, and deuotion, and with a
loud voyce aduiſed the Archbiſhop , and the other paſſen-
gers to do the ſame, with hope
to obtayne by this meanes
that , which they could not
procure by other. They did ſo
all with one voyce ,crying out
with much feeling, and many
teares, *Holy Father Ignatius re-*
*leeue vs in this our neceſſity.*Preſently in that inſtant they ſen-
ſibly perceiued the efficacy of
the Bleſſed Fathers interceſſiō.
For the wynd being at the hi-
gheſt, became preſently quiet,

and

and calme, to the great admiration and ioy of all those who were in the ship, and did now see themselues aliue, where as before they esteemed themselues but dead mē. The Archbishop promised, to celebrate yearely the feast of the Blessed Father Ignatius, saying his Masse *in Pontificalibus*, so soone as the Apostolicke Sea should canonize him : and the other passengers promised other things, euery one according to his deuotion, as appeareth by the informations made in the Citty of *Santa—fe* of that new Kingdome, before the same Archbishop Don Bartholomeo, and also in Carthagena by the authority of Don Iuan de Ladrada, of Saynt

Domi-

Dominicks order, Bishop of that Citty.

13. The Fathers Alphonsus Medranus, and Francis Figueroa, with the others that went in their company, were not deliuered only by this miracle, and at this tyme, from the euident dangers of the Sea by the intercession of Blessed Father Ignatius. For returning in the yeare 1600. from the foresaid new Kingdome of Granada, towards Spayne, in the Gallion, named *Our Lady of Arançaçu*, passing out of the straites of Bahama, they endured many, and very terrible stormes. For the tyde with them was very strong & vehement, against which encountred a contrary wynd, &

Another miracle vpon the sea.

of

of both sides they were inuiro-
ted with sands, and shallowes,
and in very great danger. Father Frauncis Figueroa cast a
Relique of the Blessed Father
into the sea, beseeching him
deuoutly to help them; which
he did in such manner, that the
sea was presently calme.

14. But this fauour from
Heauen, and the force of the
Blessed Fathers intercession appeared much more in another
greater daunger wherein they
were, neere vnto the Ilāds, called Terceras. For one morning
at the dawning of the day, so-
dainly the wind arose so furi-
ously, that it ouerturned the
Galleon, and the maryners and
passēgers seing imminent danger of death, kneeling downe,

con-

confessed their sinnes publik-
ly with a loud voice, beseeching our Lords mercy . The
wynd brake downe the greatest sayle, and those of the Galleon remembring the benefit
which they had receyued before in the channell of Bahama,
by meanes of the inuocation,
and Relique of Blessed Father
Ignatius, cryed out with great
instance to Father Francis Figueroa, desyring him to cast a-
gaine the same Relique into
the sea, that God might be pleased to deliuer them the second
tyme also from so euident dā-
ger by his intercession . The
Father did so, and presently (ô
goodnes of God, who honou-
reth his seruants in this manner !) the ayre became calme,

Y   the

the sea quiet, the sun shining,
which was before couered, &
al in the ship were comforted,
and moued to thankesgiuing,
seeing themselues free from
that feare, danger, and terror
wherein they were before, as
the same Fathers, and others
who came in the Galleon, did
testify.

15. There was a woman
in India so much inflamed
with filthy, & dishonest loue,
that nothing seemed able to
quench it. She had a Relique
of B. Father Ignatius giuen
her, & by the meanes thereof,
that Diuellish inflammation
ceased, which had almost consumed, and put her out of her
witts. And in the same māner
there haue beene many others

in

He deli-
uereth
an Indiā
woman
from
tempta-
tions a-
gainst
chastity.

in diuers Prouinces,& places, who commending themselues earneſtly to our Lord, & crauing his fauour by the merits of his ſeruant Ignatius, haue obtayned victory of their temptations, peace, and ſerenity in their ſoules, health for their bodyes, eaſe in theyr troubles,ſecurity in their dangers,and remedy in their aduerſityes.

Of the wonderfull beginning, &
Progreſſe of the Society
of I E S V S.

C H A P.   XXIIII.

BVт though the miracles, which are here related,& many other,which I omit for

breuity, be fo great, & fo certayne ; notwithftanding the
greateft of all (in my opinion)
is, that God hath chofen this
Bleffed Father to inftitute ,
gouerne, and extend an Order
of Religion , which amongft
Catholikes , Heretickes , and
Infidells , hath in fo fhort a
fpace done fo much good in
the world . And this Mi-
racle is fo great, and fo notorious, that although there
were no other , this alone
ought to be fufficiēt, to know
and efteeme the fáctity which
our Lord hath giuen to this
venerable Father . Synce it is
certayne, that when our Lord
choofeth one for any great
matter, he giueth him fuch
grace and talents , as are neceffary

ceſſary for the conuenient execution, &, accompliſhment
therof.

2. And I think that any
wiſe, and vnpaſſionate man
will iudge the ſame, if he conſider the alteration, which
God made, changing Ignatius
from a worldly, and vayne
ſouldiar, & making him Cap-
tayn of this Sacred Warfarre,
and Father of ſo many, and
ſuch eminent Children. He
that ſhal think vpon the hard
wayes, by which he guided
him, and the perſeuerance, &
victory, that he gaue him:
what company he ioyned to
him in Paris, ſome being Spaniards, and others Frenchmē,
at the very tyme that Spayne
and France were at cruell

wars:

wars: and how he vnited, and bound them together with the band of perfect charity. The persecutions, & stormes, which this Vessel hath endured, from the tyme that our Lord launched it into the sea, and that it hath alwayes arriued at a secure hauen, what wynd soeuer it had, when weak men, and such as were worldly wise, made account that it would haue perished.

3. He that shall ponder with attention the frame, and forme of the Institute of this Religion, which God inspired to this B. Father, so like in the essentiall poynts to other orders, and so vnlike in some, which are proper to it selfe. The progresse and propaga-

tion which the hand of Almighty God hath giuen vnto it, since that in sixty yeares which are past (frō the yeare 1540. in which the Pope confirmed it, vntil the yeare 1600. in which I write this history) our Lord hath multiplyed, & enlarged it throughout all the Kingdomes of Christédome, and in so many, & so remote countryes of the Indians, and barbarous people, where the light of the Ghospell had not before appeared. So that in Angola, Monacongum, Monometapa, Brasil, Ethiopia, Ormuz, Goa, Malaca, Malucas, China, and Iaponia, and in the kingdomes of Mogor, and Pegù, with others, our Fathers are resident (to omit,

Y 4   as

as more known, the firme lãd
Perù, new Spayne, the Ilands
of Manilla, or the Philip-
pines:) and the Society hath
more then three hundred, and
fifty Colledges, and Houses,
distributed into three and
twenty Prouinces, and two
vice-Prouinces.

4. He will also iudge the
same, who shall cast his eyes
vpon that which more im-
porteth, to wit, the fruit which
our Lord hath drawne out of
the labours of this B. Father,
and of his children among
Catholiks, Infidells, and Hereticks. There is no cause to
relate in this place, that which
belongeth to Catholiks, but
only to consider, & ponder it,
since that we haue it before

our eyes, and we fee, & touch with our hands the care , and follicitude , with which our Fathers imploy themfelues in teaching children the Chriftian doctrine and the youth good learning, and manners : in vifiting and comforting thofe, who are detayned in prifons, & the fick in the hofpitalls, and in releeuing the poore, and needy, & helping men to dye well.

5. And it cannot be denyed, that though the Common wealth hath fallen , and beene impayred much in other things : yet there hath been great reformation in many feruants of God , concerning preaching more profitably, and more oftner, tou-

ching prayer, and meditation
of the diuine Misteryes: the
vse, and frequentation of the
Holy Sacraments of Confession, and Communion; and
in mortification, & pennāce:
though al that is done be litle,
if we cōsider, what we ought
to do. Likewise the other orders of Religion haue been replenished with many scollers
of the Society, who perseuere,
and florish in them with great
praise, and commendation.
And these Religions them-
selues, encouraged with the
help and succour, which our
Fathers haue afforded them,
haue more discouered their
holy zeale, and extended greater beames of their sanctity,
and learning, sustayning the

Com-

Common wealth vpon their
ſhoulders, & mouing vs with
their exāple, to labour more,
and to attend with greater
vigilancy, and carefulnes, to
our miniſteryes & functions.

6. That which concer-
neth the Infidells, is ſo much,
that it cannot be explicated
in few words, neyther is it
conuenient, that we ſhould
ſpend many, in declaring,
what innumerable ſoules a-
mong the Gentills, the children of this Bleſſed Father
haue illuminated with light
from heauen, and brought to
the knowledg of Ieſus Chriſt,
and to the ſweet yoke of his
holy law: And what labours
they haue endured, and do endure to bring this to paſſe; &

how

how many, and what great
miracles God hath wrought
by them, by reason that they
were neceſſary for the plan-
ting of the faith in thoſe places. Neyther can any, who
inioy the peace, and quietnes,
that thoſe who were borne in
theſe Kingdomes do enioy
(Bleſſed be our Lord, who
giueth vs this peace, & than-
ked be our Pyous Princes
who conſerue it,) eaſely be-
leeue, vnleſſe they ſee it, what
profit our Lord hath done, &
cōtinually doth in the Kingdomes, and Prouinces infected with Hereſyes; and what
battayles, and combats our
Fathers haue with Hereticks
without intermiſſion.

7. But that, which they

who haue experience of those
countryes, say, and which we
who haue seene it, know, is
that with the exemplar life of
our Fathers, with the Catholike & sound doctrine taught
in Scholes, preached in Pul-
pits, published in printed
bookes, examined and tryed
in disputations with Heretiks
themselues, and the institutio
of the youth (which in these
prouinces only was in former
yeares to the nuber of aboue
thirty thousand schollars, and
now is far greater) the holy
Catholicke faith which seemed to be decayed and fallen
in the Northern Prouinces,
is reuiued, & hath taken head,
& recouered strégth, to resist,
couince, conquer, & triumph

over

ouer lyes, and falfehood. And
an innumerable number of
thofe which wauered , haue
been confirmed in the obedience of the Romā Church:
and many Heretiks, who had
forfaken it , haue returned to
it agayn; and thofe who con-
tinue obftinate , and blynd
for theyr intereft, and ambi-
tion , haue notwithftanding
loft their former fury ; and
feare thofe of the Society
(whome they call Iefuires)
and confeffe playnly , that
they are their vtter enemyes,
and as fuch, they abhorre,
calumniate , and perfecute
them .

8. There haue been many
Colledges , & Seminaryes e-
rected for the education of

poore

poore schollers, especially of
those, who are banished, and
suffer persecution for theyr
faith : and there lyue in them
many Priests, and Religious
men of all orders, vnder the
disciplyne, and gouerment of
the Society, who hauing ended theyr studyes, returne to
theyr Churches, and Mona-
steryes, and are profitable for
theyr reformation, and to pro-
uoke others by their examples.
And by this meanes, and by
reason, that many from the
Scholes of the Society haue
entered into Religion, the
Clergy, and the Orders of Religious themselues (which in
those parts were much de-
cayed) haue beene reformed,
and haue recouered theyr an-

cient beauty , and splendour.

9. In like manner , whole Villages , Townes , Cittyes , and Prouinces haue byn conserued in the Catholicke faith: & with Cógregations, Houses of Conuictors, Sermons , vse and frequentation of the holy Sacraments, fasting, pennances , and workes of mercy , they haue reuiued their faith , and shewed by their actions , that they are children of the Catholike Church . And that this fruit may be more durable and lasting, and more acceptable and pleasing to our Lord : the sonnes of Ignatius water these plants with their bloud, dying for the Catholik faith, and testifying by theyr death, that it is the truth; since

that

that they giue their life in defence therof For besides aboue 25 . of the Society, which in both the Indies haue sealed the preaching of the Ghospel with their bloud : more then 60. others haue dyed by the hands of Heretiks.

10. For becaufe the Hereticks abhorre fo much thofe of this religion , and thinke that by bereauing them of their liues , they fhall find leffe hinderance in their mifchiefe ; it is a very ordinary thing , to perfecute , apprehend , torment, and vfe them like Traytors, as may be feene daily, and experience it felfe hath made it manifeft . The which alfo is a great argument , that it is the worke of God , and that he

Z   who

who founded it, was chosen
by him, especially with his
owne and his childrens labours, to amplify and enlarge
the glory of the same Lord
who did chuse him, and to illustrate his holy Catholike
Church.

11. And this is (as I haue
said) the greatest, of all the miracles of this Blessed Father,
and the Miracle of Miracles,
in which are contayned so many, and so notable Miracles,
as the wonderfull things are,
which our Lord hath wrought
by him, and his children. Be
he therfore Blessed, and glori-
fyed, as the Author, and wor-
ker of all that is good: since
that (as the Apostle saith)
Neither he who planteth, is any

*thing , nor he who watereth : but
God who maketh that to encrease
and fructify , which is planted
and watered : and to whom , as
to the roote thereof , all the
beauty and fruit of the tree is
due .*

*Sundry Testimonies , of Holy men ,
of Kinges , Princes , and
Prelates , concerning B
Father Ignatius .*

CHAP. XXV.

VV E haue enlarged
our selues much , in
this life of our Blessed Father
Ignatius ; but for that we hauing knowne , and conuersed
so much with him , it hath
giuen vs leaue to exceed our

   ordi-

ordinary courſe, & indeed we
know certainly that all which
hath byn ſaid to be too litle
in reſpect of that which might
be ſaid . And becauſe as yet he
is not a Canonized Saint , nor
propoſed to the whole Church
by the holy Apoſtolick Sea to
be inuocated, and reuerenced,
as the others ate, whoſe lyues
we haue written : it hath bin
neceſſary to relate ſome more
particuler things, & miracles,
which in the liues of other
Saints might be for breuity
well omitted . Though it be
certayne , that we pretermit
many other , eſteeming theſe
ſufficient for that which we
pretend in writing this life:
that is , to glorify our Lord,
who hath made him a Saint,

to difcouer his vertues , for
our example : and that they
who are ignorant of them ,
may come to know them ,
and conceiue deuotion to-
wards this holy Father .

2 . And for this caufe before I make an end, I will add,
that as this Bleffed Father was
a Saynt in his life , fo he was
knowne , efteemed , and reuerenced for a Saynt by all
thofe , who treated with him,
and much more by them, who
were more familiarly acquainted with him, becaufe they did
fee more neerely his admirable
vertues , and touched , as it
were , with their hand , the
great gifts , and graces which
God had endued him withall .

3 . Father Frauncis Xauier

all

an Apostolicall man, and of
such rare sanctity, by whom
God wrought so many, and
great miracles, who illustrated
innumerable Gentils, bare so
great deuotion, and reuerence
to Father Ignatius, that he did
carry a subscription of his in
his bosome, as a firme buckler
against all dangers. And from
the remote Countryes of India, he wrote letters vnto him,
vpon his knees.

4. Father Peter Faber,
who was the first that ioyned
with him, in the erection of the
Society, an admirable man,
and of maruelous diuine illu-
strations; tooke Father Ignatius for his patterne, and example of Holynes, and of all
vertue.

5. Father Iames Laynes, the second Generall of the Society, and a man so much esteemed in the world, for his great learning and religion, told me, that because God was so much pleased, with the soule of his Seruant Ignatius, he did so much good to the Society, and so greatly fauoured the children therof.

6. Father Frauncis Borgia, the third Generall of the Society, a man so well knowne to the world, by reason of his Nobility, and much more of his Sanctity, went to Rome the yeare 1550. principally to see, know, and conuerse with Blessed Father Ignatius. And when he said his first Masse, (which was in the

houſe of Loyola) he kiſſed
the floore of the Chamber
where the Father was borne,
by reaſon of the great deuotion , which he bare vnto
him , as vnto ſo holy a man .
And this was the opinion of
all others who treated familiarly with him . But not only thoſe who liued with him,
had this eſtimation of his ſanctity , but likewiſe thoſe a-
broad had the ſame conceit
and reſpect of him in like
manner .

7. Pope Paul the third, of
bleſſed Memory , who was
the firſt that confirmed the
Society , did very many important things by the coun-
ſayle of this Bleſſed Father;
and among others , one was

to

to inftitute in Rome the fu-
preme Counfell of the Inquifi-
fition, and to appoynt foure
moft graue Cardinalls to haue
care of matters belonging to
the Catholick faith, in that
holy Tribunail.

8. Pope Iulius the third
would not make Father Peter
Canifius Bifhop of Vienna,
as the King of the Romans
Don Ferdinand requefted very earneftly, becaufe B. Father Ignatius would not giue
his confent therto : fo great
was the refpect, which the
Pope bare vnto him.

9. Pope Marcellus the
fecond, who fucceeded to Iulius the third, faid : That in
matters of the Society, the
authority of Father Ignatius

Z 5 alone

alone was of more weight
with him ; then all the reasons , which could be allead-
ged to the contrary .

10. Pope Paul the fourth ,
(in the tyme of whose Pope-
dome the Blessed Father departed ,) honoured him so
much , that when he spake
with him , he bad him rise
vp, and couer his head.

11. Pope Gregory the 13.
in the Bulls which he graunted the yeare of our Lord 1582.
and 1583 . in confirmation
and defence ,of the Institute
of the Society , expresly saith ,
That the holy Ghost inspired
Ignatius to institute the Society, and to prescribe the forme,
which the Institute thereof
contayneth . He saith more ,

That

That all the Chriſtian Common wealth is eaſed , and re-
freſhed by the children of the
Society .

12. And he, and his Pre-
deceſſors Pius I I I I. and Pius
v. do ſo exceedingly , and
with ſuch exaggeration ,praiſe
and extoll the miniſteryes,
and functions of the Society ,
and the fruite which God
hath drawne , and daily dra-
weth out of them , that for
modeſty I will not relate them
in this place : but all this fruit
proceeded (as from the roote
thereof,) from Ignatius , by
the aſſiſtance of our Lords
grace .

13. The King of the Ro-
mans (whom we named be-
fore) Don Ferdinando , be-

fides the Colledges of the Society which he founded, and his great fauour towards vs in respect of B. Father Ignatius, being much inclyned to make Father Claudius Iayus (one of the first Fathers) Bishop of Trieste, he did it not, vnderstanding that Father Ignatius was of a contrary opinion, and did not like it.

14. Don Iohn the third, King of Portugall, by reason of the great deuotion which he bare to this Bleſſed Father, commaunded Father Lewis Gonzales de Camera, when he went from Portugall to Rome, in the yeare 1553. to be attentiue, and conſider all the actions of Father Ignatius, and write them in particuler

to

to him . Which the Father did,
and wrote to the King, that
concerning the matter, which
he had commended vnto him,
he was not so much in-
flamed in the loue of God, by
any spirituall readinge , or
prayer , as by the attention ,
which he vsed in behoulding
Father Ignatius.

15. The Cardinall Don
Gaspar de Quiroga, Archbishop of Toledo, and Generall
Inquisitor in the Kingdomes
of Spayne , who in Rome had
byn the said Fathers great
friend , testifyeth of him, that
he was a most perfect man ,
truly humble , meeke , patient
a despiser of the world , and
inflamed with the zeale of
Gods glory, and the good of
soules.

foules : and that he was neuer
troubled, nor changed countenance, for any variety of prof-
perity, or aduerfity.

16. Cardinall Gabriel
Paleotto, Bifhop of Bono-
nia, calleth him, The light
of the Church : and faith,
That God moued him to in-
ftitute the Society, for the greater ftrengthening, and for-
tifying, of Ecclefiafticall dif
cipilne.

17. The Duke of Bauaria,
Albertus, was very much a-
dicted to Bleffed Father Ignatius, and wrote vnto him
many tymes, and reuerenced
him as a Saint, and for his refpect imbraced, and tauoured
his children, as his Succeffors
haue done euer fince ; who

haue

haue inherited no leffe the Piety of theyr Aunceftors, then the Greatnes of their Houfe.

18. The Prefident of Caftilla, Iohn Vega, being Embaffadour for the Emperour Charles the fifth, in Rome; held very great friendfhip with the Father; and in a letter which he wrote to the Society, at the tyme of his difceafe, he called him *Bleffed*, and *Holy Captaine*, and worthy to haue his banner placed in Heauen, with thofe of S Dominick, and S. Francis.

19. Maifter Iohn of Aquila, an Apoftolicall Preacher, (whofe life was written by Father Lewis of Granada, deferuing fo excellent a Recorder)

corder) said of his humility,
That Blessed Father Ignatius
was a Giant, and he in his
comparison but a dwarfe.

20. The same Father
Lewis of Granada, speaking
of the Blessed Father, saith:
That he meruailed at the life,
heroyical, and most admirable
vertues of that new Mirrour
of Vertue, & Prudence, which
God had sent vnto the world
in our tymes, for the saluation
of infinite soules. So are his
wordes.

21. And in this manner
do many other very wise,
and graue men think, and
speak. And many authors of
Diuers nations, who haue
written since the Society began, do speak of him as of an
Holy

Holy man : As Laurence Surius a Germane by Nation, who briefly writeth his life. And Iohn Molanus of Flaunders, who calleth him, *Most Blessed*. And Genebrard a French-man, who saith, That God sent him against Luther. And Doctour Nicolas Saunders, an Englishman, who calleth him, A man of God, and moued by our Lord to do the worke, which he performed. Thomas Bozius nameth him, A most famous man for the sactity of his life. Paulus Morigia, of the Order of the Iesuati, and Angelus del Paz, of S. Francis Order, and Mambrinus Rosa, all foure Italian Authors, write, and commend the life

A a　　　　of

Origine
relig. c.
77.
Angelus
in tract.
de præ-
pof. ad
commun.
p.121.
Mambri.
in hift.
l.3.
Ygles.c.
2,part.
hift.Pon-
tific. lib.
6.in vita
Pauli 3.
Villeg.
tom.1. in
vita Ign.
Garibay
hift. Hif-
pan,l.30.
cap.5.
Paiua l.
1.orthod.
inftit.

of the Bleffed Father. And
Gonzales de Yglefças, and
Maifter Alphonfus of Vil-
legas, and Stephen of Garibay, Spanifh Hiftoriogra-
phers of our tyme, write the
fame of him, and call him,
Bleffed, *Happy*, and *Saynt*.
And Doctor Iames of Paiua,
a Portugefe (who as a Doctor
of Diuinity for his King, was
prefent in the Councell of
Trent)nameth him an *Illuftri-*
ous example of Sanctity, An admirable man,and giuen to the
world for a particuler benefit
from heauen.

22. And if we turne our
eyes to the Kings, and Princes, who accounting him a
Saynt, haue befeeched our
moft holy Father Pope Cle-

ment

ment the eight, that this day
sitteth into the chayre of S.
Peter, to declare him to be so,
and to put him into the Cata-
logue of Saynts; we shall find,
that the greatest, and most
mighty Princes of Christen-
dome, haue desired, and beseeched it with great instance.
For the Emperour Rodulphus
the second of his name, and
the Empresse Doña Maria of
Austria his mother, and the
Catholick King Philip the second of glorious memory, and
King Philip the 3. his Sonne,
who raigneth at this day, togeather with Queene Mar-
garet, and Duke William of
Bauaria, the Archdutchesse
Doña Maria his sister, and
others, haue written letters to

his Holynesse, in which they
call him Blessed, and Holy Father, and from whose most
Holy, and Religious life, as
from their fountayne, the
current of many gifts, and
graces hath reioyced the Citty
of God.

23. And not only these,
and other great Princes haue
shewed their piety and deuotion, which they beare to the
Father, making intercession
for his Canonization; but also
whole Kingdomes haue done
the same: as that of Castilla in
their Parlament; that of Aragon, that of Valentia, and the
Princedome of Cataluña,
with their Viceroyes, and Go-
uernours; the holy Churches
of Toledo, Ciuill, Granada,

and

and Corduba; the Cittyes of
Saragoza, Valencia, and Bar-
celona, and the Prouince of
Guipuzcoa (where the Father
was borne) and many other
Biſhops, Dukes, and Lords.

24. And this is the com-
mon conſent, and opinion of
Chriſtian, wiſe, and vnpaſſionate men of all Nations:
only the Hereticks thinke, and
ſpeake euill of this Bleſſed Father, and write bookes againſt
his life, and againſt his Religion; as a great Caluiniſt he-
reticke hath done, named Symon Lithus Miſſenus, who
wrote fiue bookes againſt the
other fiue of his life, which
are in print; which is no leſſe
teſtimony of his Sanctity,
then the praiſe, which ſo ma-

A a 3 ny,

ny, and so graue men, that haue byn heere recited, do giue him. For as it is a great praise, to be praised by the good; so it is no lesse, to be dispraised by the bad, as S. Hierome saith, writing to S. Augustine in these words. *The Catholickes reuerence, and admire you, as the repayrer, and restorer of the ancient faith, and that which is a signe of greater glory, all Hereticks hate, and reuile you: and they persecute me with the same malice, killing in desire those, whom they cannot bereaue of their life with the sword.*

FINIS.